A Taste of
CUBA

A Taste of
CUBA

Beatriz Llamas

Translated by Claudia Lightfoot
Illustrations by Ximena Maier

Interlink Books
An imprint of Interlink Publishing Group, Inc.
New York • Northampton

First published in 2005 by
INTERLINK BOOKS
An imprint of Interlink Publishing Group, Inc.
46 Crosby Street
Northampton, Massachusetts 01060
www.interlinkbooks.com

ISBN 1–56656–553–7

Text © Beatriz Llamas 2005
Translation © Claudia Lightfoot 2005
Illustrations © Ximena Maier 2005
Photographs © Michael Bonaparte 2005
Design © Macmillan Publishers Limited 2005

Designed by Gary Fielder at AC Design
Cover design by Gary Fielder at AC Design
Food styling by Wendy Rahamut

Printed in Thailand

2009 2008 2007 2006 2005
10 9 8 7 6 5 4 3 2 1

Contents

Chapter 1

The Cuban table

Cuban cuisine is an accumulation of methods and ingredients drawn from both the island's history and its natural resources. As the Cuban gastronome and writer Reynaldo González said: "The history of our cuisine began when the native Indians had been eliminated and everything apart from the landscape itself had to be imported into Cuba, initially mainly by Europeans and then by ever-increasing numbers of enslaved Africans. Just as blood and skin color mingled so did flavors and seasonings. What is more, even if blood and skin had not become obviously mixed, flavors and seasonings would have fused in any case as the inevitable result of the marriage of ancient cultures giving rise to the gestation of a new one". (*Echale salsita!*, Editorial Lo Real Maravilloso, La Habana, 2000. p.7)

When the Spanish arrived on the island in 1492, they met with an indigenous population that lived mainly by fishing, a little hunting and some sparse cultivation of cassava, sweet potato, corn, and black beans. When the aboriginal population disappeared as a result of the new illnesses and living conditions brought in by the colonizers, these foodstuffs gave way to those of Spanish influence. Virtually the only dish to have survived from that era is casabe, a kind of bread made of cassava that has been grated, strained, formed into cake shapes and grilled on iron griddles. Not only did the Spanish bring many ingredients to the local cuisine but they also introduced many cooking methods and dishes that acquired local characteristics once they had taken hold in Cuba.

The second major influence on Cuban cooking was the arrival of the African slaves, brought over by the new colonists to undertake the hardest physical labor. With the slaves came mainly agricultural products such as okra, taro root, and plantain. These are such important elements of Cuban cuisine nowadays that it seems as though they have always been present on the island. The fact that slaves also worked in the plantation kitchens meant that they introduced some of their own tastes and culinary methods to the tables of the ruling classes. The new and growing slave population created the need for the cultivation of new products with which to feed them. It is possible that the cultivation of rice in Cuba was established in order to meet this new demand.

Two other events in Cuban history have had an influence on Cuban culinary customs, albeit minor. At the end of the eighteenth century, plantation owners of French origin arrived from Haiti, fleeing the slave revolts there. They established themselves mainly in the east of the island and many of them took up the cultivation of coffee as they had done in Haiti, thus increasing Cuban production enormously. Unlike sugar cane, coffee plants need trees to shade them, and more skill and delicacy in their cultivation. While the sugar plantation owners tended to arrive only at harvest time, the majority of coffee planters lived on their estates and tended them like gardens. Their homes too had an atmosphere of refinement and sophistication. The abundant fruit trees that shaded the coffee plants, along with the meticulously maintained vegetable gardens and stockyards, served to contribute to a more elegant and discriminating table. These new immigrants brought customs to Cuba such as the use of pepper, and dishes such as stuffed rolled roasts of meat.

The other significant historical event was the arrival of Chinese immigrants in the middle of the nineteenth century. They came to Cuba in conditions of semi-slavery and brought with them soy sauce, rice prepared in the Chinese style, and sweet and sour flavorings.

The rich and powerful classes in Cuba in the nineteenth and first half of the twentieth centuries clearly favored both French cuisine and cooks who were either from France itself or trained in French cooking. In general though, they never stopped appreciating and serving local dishes such as ajiaco at their tables.

Soups and stews form an important part of the Cuban diet and many of these have their roots in the Spanish influence. *El ajiaco*, a soup or stew derived from the classic Spanish "pot au feu" *olla podrida* but using local ingredients, is one example of this. Considered to be the national dish of Cuba, this stew is made from various vegetables such as taro root, cassava, sweet potato, corn, yam, squash, and plantain boiled with pork, chicken, or dried beef. Finally it is flavored with sofrito and served with lime wedges. Sofrito, a mixture of onion, garlic, green peppers, and tomatoes sautéed in oil, is the basic Cuban seasoning, to which other spices such as cumin, oregano, and cilantro are often added. It is said that Cuban culture itself is an "ajiaco", referring to the mixture of races and cultures on the island that fuse into one single whole.

Thick vegetable broths in the Spanish style are also served daily with white rice at the Cuban table. White, black, or kidney beans as well as dried peas are most often used for these broths.

Stews can either be based around vegetables or cereals flavored with meat or fish, or be primarily of beef, poultry, or fish and seasoned with vegetables or simply a sofrito. The point is that the sauce from these stews is essential to "wet" the rice eaten daily in Cuba. Classic examples include stews prepared with the delicious shellfish that is found in abundance around the island's shores: lobster or shrimp cooked with chili and seasoned with a sofrito and white wine – *enchilada de*

langosta o camarones. There is also okra stew with plantain dumplings, and chicken "Rancho Luna" marinated in garlic and sour orange, two basic flavorings in Cuban stews.

Okra and plantain, both plants of African origin, were always favorite ingredients of the slaves in the colonial era and both continue to be enormously popular. So much so that in one way or another, fried, or boiled and sprinkled with *mojo de ajo*, a garlic, oil, and sour orange sauce, plantain is served every day. The slaves' diet consisted basically of dried beef and salt cod served with vegetables and cereals such as corn and rice. Cuba was at one time a great producer of dried beef but the extensive cultivation of sugar cane in the nineteenth century squeezed out the beef farms. Dried beef then began to be imported by the colonists, as was salt cod and many other ingredients of Cuban cooking. The beef and cod provided cheap and easily preserved forms of protein in the hot climate. Curiously, nowadays both are luxury products at inaccessible prices and much yearned for by Cubans.

Cubans' favorite meats are chicken and pork. Roast leg of pork or suckling pig marinated in sour orange, cumin, garlic, oregano, and salt is the main dish at all major feasts and celebrations. The most popular nowadays is New Year's Eve, and for December 31 a leg of pork or suckling pig is roasted and served with congrí rice (rice cooked with black beans), fried plantain, and cassava with *mojo de ajo*, together with salad and followed by some traditional desserts.

The reason why rice is eaten so often and widely in Cuba is unclear, but certainly a meal without rice is not considered by Cubans to be complete. The rice is served either simply boiled to be mixed with the sauce or gravy from the accompanying broth or in specific rice dishes. The rice in these dishes tends to have an orangey color, derived from annatto seeds (*bijol*) and the tomatoes in the sofrito, and is often called "yellow rice". These dishes are flavored with meat, fish, vegetables, or combinations of all three and, apart from a substantial broth, it is always essential to add a good sofrito. Rice dishes are very traditional and popular in Cuban cuisine, from dishes such as chicken and rice "a la Chorrera" to congrí rice cooked with black or kidney beans, or the more subtle and less well-known dish of rice with green bananas.

Fried food is the other mainstay of Cuban cuisine and many types of fritters are served: corn, black-eyed beans, cod, taro root, chickpeas, squash … Most of these fritters involve mixing the main ingredient with beaten egg and possibly garlic, onion, or parsley. There are also crunchy fritters made of taro root or plantain cut very finely and fried until they resemble potato chips, as well as all manner of fried croquettes and small pies.

In Spanish, "*vianda*" means food or nutrition generally, but in Cuba the word applies specifically to a group of tubers and vegetables that are normally fried or boiled and served with a sauce or seasoning. Among them are cassava, taro root, sweet potato, squash, potatoes, plantains, yams, chayote, etc.

No Cuban meal is served without a salad, and frequently the salad includes both fruit and vegetables. Avocado, tomato, cucumber, cabbage, beetroot, pineapple, papaya, watercress, lettuce … all are mixed in various ways and well dressed with oil and vinegar or with a flavored mayonnaise. Chicken or shellfish are often added to the mixture. Pulses, although less frequently used in salads, can be dressed in this way too, so salads of chickpeas, black and black-eyed beans are also sometimes served.

And finally, let us talk of sweet things, which, in this land of sugar, are sacred. There is no fine Cuban meal that does not end with a delicious dessert, a coffee, cigar, and rum. Among the wide range of desserts those based on fruit and sugar are always very popular. So we have guava jam, guava paste and guavas in syrup, all normally accompanied by a mild cheese; orange and grapefruit peel in syrup; the little coconut cones

so typical of the city of Baracoa; or *atropellado matancero*, made with pineapple and coconut in syrup. There are also desserts made from tubers, such as boniatillo where sweet potato is the main ingredient, or from vegetables, such as squash pudding, as well as those made from rice or corn and eggs and milk. The list of Cuban desserts is endless.

This book presents a selection of Cuban dishes from all periods. Many recipes have come from kind friends, some are old classics and others are new recreations. I want to thank the many friends who have helped me and I hope that you all enjoy this "sketch" of the Cuban cuisine.

Chapter 2

Ingredients in Cuban cooking

Alcaparrado

A mixture of raisins, olives, and capers used to season certain dishes.

Aniseed

Both *Pimpinella anisum* and *Illicium verum* (star anise) varieties are used. If the seeds of *Pimpinella anisum* are used they can be whole or ground.

Annatto seeds (achiote y bijol)

Bixa orellana

The seeds of the annatto tree are commercially manufactured into a food colorant, called "*bijol*" in Spanish. One can turn the seeds into colorant at home by heating some oil in a skillet without letting it boil, pouring it over some annatto seeds and letting them soak in the oil for 1 or 2 days. The oil will take on a red color from the seeds. Strain the oil and keep it in the refrigerator. Annatto oil is used only to give food color; it adds no flavor.

Banana leaves

Banana leaves are used to wrap tamales and bacanes. The leaves should be trimmed to the size indicated and blanched in boiling water before use to make them pliable.

Bananas and plantains

- Banana (*Musa paradisiaca*): sometimes cooked when green for dishes such as bacán. There is also a variety of small, creamy fleshed banana that tastes of apples, called "little apple banana."

- Plantain (*Musa balsisiana*): plantains, though similar to bananas, more closely resemble a vegetable in flavor and texture and can only be eaten cooked. Plantains are used for different dishes according to their degree of maturity: green, when the skin is completely green and the flesh hard; speckled, when the skin has both green and yellow patches and the flesh is softer; mature when the skin is yellow and the flesh has a yellow tinge.

Black beans

Phaseolus vulgaris

Small, round, completely black beans.

Black-eyed beans

Vigna unguiculata or *vigna sinensis*

Small, round, white beans with a black spot or "eye."

Butternut squash

Cucurbita sp.

A round or gourd-shaped vegetable with green and yellow skin and orange flesh.

Casabe

A flat, dry cake made of cassava that has been grated, strained, and sieved, then formed into circles and cooked on an iron griddle. Casabe is used as a substitute for bread. Flour made from cassava that has been grated, strained to extract the juice, and sieved is also known as "*catibia*."

Cassava

Manioc esculenta

This elongated, grayish mottled tuber has fibrous white flesh that is rich in carbohydrates. Uncooked, cassava flesh contains a cyanide derivative toxin that is eliminated either by cooking or by grating it and extracting the juice. Cassava can be kept only a very short time after harvesting. In Cuba, cassava is always known as yuca.

Chayote or christophene

Sechium edule

This vegetable is part of the squash family and is shaped like a large pepper with a smooth pale green or whitish skin. The flesh is white and very watery with an edible seed inside. Chayote is used with meat in stews, on its own, or as an ingredient in desserts.

Cilantro

Coriandrum sativum

An aromatic herb resembling parsley but with an intense and very distinct flavor. It is used as a seasoning.

Coconut

Cocos nucifera

The white flesh of this tropical fruit is used in Cuba mainly for desserts. Some dishes use the coconut milk as well, made by soaking the grated flesh in water then squeezing out the liquid. See, for example, the recipe for Coquimol (page 114). Coconut water is also drunk on its own as a refreshing beverage.

Corn

Corn is used in different ways in Cuba:

- Tender corn flour is the paste made from fresh, raw, ground, or milled, corn kernels.

- Corn flour (cornmeal) or dried corn flour is the flour obtained from grinding dried corn kernels. It is yellow and rather grainy.

- Raw corn: raw corn kernels.

- Cooked corn: cooked corn kernels.

- *Maicena*: fine white flour obtained from the industrialized milling of cornstarch.

Cumin

Ground cumin is used as a seasoning.

Dried beef (jerk beef)

This is dried salted beef.

Dry cooking wine (vino seco)

Wine made from grapes and other fruit and used only for cooking. It is light brown in color, dry, and very strongly flavored. Vino seco is a particularly Cuban ingredient, uncommon in other parts of the world. It can be substituted by white wine with a few drops of vinegar added or by white wine mixed with sherry.

Fats and oils

In previous times, because of the Spanish influence, the most commonly used cooking oil in Cuba was olive oil imported from Spain. Nowadays, sunflower oil is more usually used as it is much more reasonably priced. In this book, if the recipe does not specifically indicate a type of oil, either sunflower or olive oil may be used. Olive oil is particularly good for fritters, producing better results.

Pork fat was and is also very often used for cooking.

Guava

Psidium guajava

This tropical fruit is shaped somewhat like a large plum; its skin can be pale green or yellowish and the firm but grainy flesh is either white or pink depending on the variety. The heart of the fruit is full of small, inedible seeds. Guava is eaten raw or cooked with sugar in several different ways. It is very aromatic and rich in vitamin C. The most common variety eaten in Cuba is the pink-fleshed variety known as "*cotorrera*".

Jerk beef (see Dried beef)

Lime

Citrus aurantifolia

The lime, or Caribbean lemon, is a small, smooth-skinned, green citrus fruit. The juice of the lime has an intense and acidic flavor and is much used to flavor dishes and in the preparation of cocktails.

Mint

Mentha

The variety of mint used in Cuba, *Mentha nemerosa*, has a fresh, fruity taste that gives a unique flavor to cocktails.

Okra

Hibiscus esculentus

A vegetable of African origin, okra has the shape of a chili, measures between 3 and 5 inches, and has dark green or purple skin. The flesh is a tender mass of edible seeds. When cooked, okra secrete a viscous liquid that is eliminated by adding a few drops of lemon, vinegar, or some other acid.

Olives

Green olives are the type used in Cuban cooking.

Oregano

Oregano belongs to the Lamiaceae botanical family and there are many different varieties. In Cuba there grows a variety that has fleshy, hairy, oval leaves and is used fresh. Other varieties are also used, both fresh and dried. If dried oregano is used instead of fresh, only half the amount is needed as the flavor is more intense.

Papaya

Carica papaya

A large, irregular oval-shaped tropical fruit that resembles a melon. Papayas can weigh between 8 ounces and 4 pounds. The skin of the fruit is smooth and green, and the flesh is yellow or orange in color.

Paprika

Capsicum annuum

Dried, powdered red peppers. There are both hot and sweet types but in Cuba sweet paprika is used.

Peppers

In Cuba, only sweet bell peppers are used in cooking. Among the varieties of pepper are:

- Green bell pepper (*Capsicum annuum*): used as a vegetable or seasoning.
- Red bell pepper (*Capsicum annuum*): used as a vegetable or seasoning.
- Scotch bonnet or cachucha pepper (*Capsicum chinense*): used as a flavoring and decoration.

Plantains (see Bananas)

Pork

Pork is particularly tasty in Cuba, especially when the animal has been fed on *palmiche*, the fruit of the royal palm tree. Pork meat is eaten fresh, smoked, or dried. Pork fat is used for frying, stewing, and baking.

Rice

Nowadays most of the rice consumed in Cuba comes from Asia, but originally rice would have been either a locally grown Creole variety or an import from Valencia in Spain. Cuban rice dishes should use one or other of these two. Creole rice is a medium-grained variety that needs to be cooked in an amount of water equal to its own volume; Valencian rice is round grained and is usually cooked in twice its own volume of water.

Saffron

Crocus sativus

Saffron is the stigma of a type of crocus. It is used as a flavoring but also adds color.

Scallions or spring onions

Allium cepa

The scallion is a young tender onion that has not yet developed a full bulb. It is used more as a flavoring or aromatic than a vegetable. The whole onion is used, both white and green parts.

Serrated cilantro

Eryngium foetidum

A variety of cilantro with large leaves (2–3 inches in length) that have serrated edges. The flavor is similar to that of the "parsley-leaved" cilantro but less intense. It is very often used as a seasoning in Cuba.

Sofrito

Sofrito is the basic seasoning used in many Cuban dishes and is made up of onion, garlic, green peppers, and tomatoes, chopped and lightly sautéed in oil. Different herbs and spices such as cumin, oregano, cilantro, and parsley are added according to the dish it is to season. Sometimes lard is also added to the mixture.

Sour orange

Citrus aurantium

The sour orange is a citrus fruit which has juice with an acidic but not bitter flavor. The juice is an indispensable ingredient in Cuban cuisine and the peel is also used in desserts.

Soursop

Annona muricata

This large, oval fruit with granulated skin comes from the botanical family of Annonaceae. The white flesh is very creamy and packed with inedible black seeds. The custard apple (*Annona squamosa*) and cherimoya (*Annona chirimola*), both from the same family, are also much used in Cuba, either on their own or as flavorings for ice creams or milk shakes.

Soy sauce

An Asian flavoring much used in Cuban cooking that clearly arrived with the Chinese immigrants in the middle of the nineteenth century.

Sugar cane
Saccharum officinarum

Sugar cane is principally used for the production of sugar and rum. There is also a freshly squeezed cane drink called "*guarapo*". Cubans living in the countryside like to chew pieces of cane. In this book, fresh sugar cane is used for Tuna with Sugar Cane and Coconut Glaze (page 62).

Sweet potato
Ipomoea batatas

A sweet-flavored tuber that resembles the potato, with a thick pinkish or yellowish brown skin and white flesh. Sweet potatoes can be kept for some time in a cool dark place.

Taro root
Colocasia esculenta

A fibrous, white-fleshed, brown-skinned tuber that resembles the potato. Taro root is rich in fiber, carbohydrates, proteins, and minerals and is very easily digested. Taro root can be kept for up to 2 weeks in a cool place.

Tomatoes

Tomatoes can be added to the sofrito in two different ways:

- Fresh tomato: ripe tomatoes peeled, seeded, drained, and chopped into small pieces.

- Tomato paste: paste made from crushed ripe tomatoes. Where paste is called for, it is best to use the commercially produced variety with intense red color and concentrated flavor.

Vanilla
Vanilla planifolia

Vanilla is used to flavor and give aroma to desserts. It is the edible fruit of an orchid native to the tropical areas of the Americas. Vanilla is processed and sold in pods, as natural essence, or as a powder, and can be used equally well in all three forms. Synthetic vanilla extract is also available but the quality is very much inferior to

natural vanilla. If vanilla pods are used, they should be infused in warm liquid to release their aroma.

Viandas

Viandas is the name given in Cuba to the group of tubers, greens, and fruits that are usually used as accompanying vegetables or garnish, normally boiled or fried. The group includes cassava, taro root, sweet potato, plantain, potatoes, yams, squash, and chayote.

Wheat flour

Wheat is not grown in Cuba and "flour" was traditionally made from corn or one or other of the tubers. Wheat flour arrived with the Spaniards and was known as "flour of Castille".

Yam
Dioscorea sp.

A large tuber with thick rough skin. There are many varieties, and one type can reach a weight of up to 20 pounds. The variety most often found in Cuba has a whitish flesh. Yams can be kept for a long time in a cool dark place. They should not be eaten raw as they are toxic unless cooked.

Chapter 3

Hors d'oeuvres and snacks

BLACK-EYED BEAN FRITTERS

Bollitos de carita

These fritters are made from black-eyed beans, the round white beans with a small black dot. They are often sold by vendors at the roadside.

For 20–25 fritters

Ingredients

1 ¼ cups black-eyed beans
1 teaspoon baking soda
3 garlic cloves
oil for deep frying

Method

Soak the beans overnight in water and the baking soda. The following day, drain the beans, wash them well, and rub them between your hands to remove the skins. (As long as the beans are young and tender they do not need to be boiled.)

Crush the peeled beans in a food mixer or blender with the garlic and some salt. The result should be of a creamy consistency. If the mixture looks too thick, add some water. Pour the mixture into a bowl and whisk vigorously for 10–15 minutes. This whisking process is necessary for the beans to expand and rise when they are fried. (The addition of an egg and a raising agent such as yeast will also ensure the right effect.)

Heat the oil in a skillet on a high heat. Add spoonfuls of the mixture to the pan to form the fritters. Deep fry until golden brown on both sides, then drain on kitchen paper and serve.

GREEN PLANTAIN CHIPS

Chicharritas de platano verde

Plantain, cooked in one way or another, is served almost daily at the Cuban table. It is as strong a presence in the diet as the banana palm is in the Cuban landscape, and it is hard to believe that it has not always been present here. So much so that a Cuban school history text book used to show an indigenous Indian watching Columbus's arrival at the island by sea from under a banana palm. The truth is that this plant came to Cuba from Africa after the island's discovery.

These chips are very fine slices of plantain fried until they are the consistency of crisp crackers. They are delicious served either as an appetizer or as a garnish to main dishes.

For 4 people

Ingredients

1 green plantain
olive oil for deep frying

Method

Score narrow strips lengthwise along the plantain, which can then be peeled. If you try to peel a plantain like a banana, the flesh will come away in chunks. Slice the plantain very finely into circles with a knife or slicer.

Deep fry the slices in hot oil until they are crisp and toasted golden. Remove from heat and drain on paper towel. Sprinkle with salt before serving.

> **The chips can be kept for several days in a sealed container.**

PORK CRACKLING

Chicharrones

There are two kinds of pork crackling or scratchings: *de viento* (airy scratchings), made with pork skin, and *de empella* (lard scratchings), made with pork belly fat and skin. They are delicious served as an aperitif with a mojito, and they are also sometimes added to other dishes such as plantain fufú or congrí rice. The pork scratchings made in Havana's Bodeguita Del Medio are as delicious as their famous mojitos.

Airy scratchings

Chicharrones de viento

For 12–14 scratchings

Ingredients

8 ounces pork skin
1 1/2 teaspoons salt
oil for deep frying

Method

Using a spoon, remove all traces of fat attached to the pork skin, which must be completely fat free.

Heat the oven to 250° F. Sprinkle the salt over the skin and place on a rack in the oven for 5 or 6 hours until completely dry and hard. In the past this would have been done by drying the pork skin in the sun.

Once the pork has cooled, cut the dried skin into pieces approximately 1 inch square.

Heat the oil in a skillet on a low heat. Deep fry the scratchings until they are soft and put them on a plate. Once they have all softened, turn the oil to a high heat and fry 2–3 pieces of scratchings at a time until they swell with air and turn golden. Drain on paper towel and serve.

Lard scratchings

Chicharrones de empella

For 8–10 scratchings

Ingredients

6 ounces pork belly fat with skin attached
2 tablespoons oil or pork lard
1/2 teaspoon salt

Method

Cut the bacon into 1/2 inch thick slices and then into approximately 1 inch squares.

Place the pieces into a skillet with the oil or pork fat and fry on a medium heat for 20–25 minutes until they have released half their fat and begun to turn golden. At this moment they should be swimming in their own fat. Dissolve the salt in a tablespoon of water, add to the skillet, raise the heat and continue frying until all the water has evaporated and the scratchings are golden. Drain on paper towel and serve.

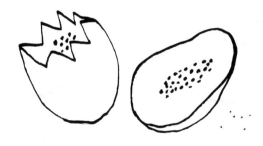

For best results the skin and lard should be from a young, tender pig.

The fat left over from frying the scratchings can be used to cook other recipes that use pork fat.

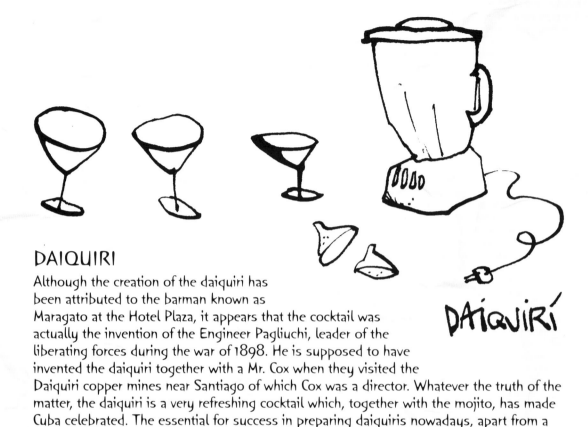

DAIQUIRI

Although the creation of the daiquiri has been attributed to the barman known as Maragato at the Hotel Plaza, it appears that the cocktail was actually the invention of the Engineer Pagliuchi, leader of the liberating forces during the war of 1898. He is supposed to have invented the daiquiri together with a Mr. Cox when they visited the Daiquiri copper mines near Santiago of which Cox was a director. Whatever the truth of the matter, the daiquiri is a very refreshing cocktail which, together with the mojito, has made Cuba celebrated. The essential for success in preparing daiquiris nowadays, apart from a good 3-year-old rum and freshly squeezed lime, is a blender powerful enough to crush the ice very finely. In Havana, the daiquiris made at the Floridita bar are delicious and are served with equally delicious taro root and plantain chips.

For 2 people

Ingredients

¼ cup 3-year-old rum
juice of ½ lime
2 teaspoons sugar
3–4 ice cubes

Method

Put all the ingredients into a blender and blend until they reach the consistency of a creamy sorbet. Serve in martini glasses.

SQUASH FRITTERS WITH RAISINS AND PEANUTS

Frituras de calabaza con pasas y mani

After the discovery of America in 1492, the flow of immigrants to Cuba from Spain did not cease until well into the twentieth century. They brought with them customs and products that grew to form an inseparable part of Creole culture, including their language. Spanish olive oil is one of the products that has become a central element of Cuban cuisine despite the fact that it will always be imported. That is why it is impossible to conceive of a Creole black bean broth or a dish of raw marinated fish without a dash of olive oil. The same is true for fritters— the most delicious are fried in olive oil, although nowadays other cheaper oils are also used.

For 20–25 fritters

Ingredients

13 ounces squash, seeded and peeled
1 teaspoon wheat flour
2 eggs
¼ cup shelled roasted peanuts
2 tablespoons raisins, soaked in water for 20 minutes
olive oil for deep frying

Method

Boil the squash in water for approximately 20–25 minutes until tender. Drain well, place in a bowl, and mash with a fork until it reaches the consistency of a purée.

Sprinkle the flour over the mashed squash and mix in well. Add the beaten eggs, peanuts, and the drained raisins. Mix all the ingredients together and season with salt.

Heat the oil in a small skillet and drop in spoonfuls of the mixture. Deep fry until golden, then drain on paper towel.

— 19 —

TARO ROOT FRITTERS

Frituras de malanga

The taro root is a most important tuber in the Cuban diet. A Cuban mother will not consider her children to be properly nourished without taro root, which is often one of the first solids offered to babies being weaned. Boiled taro root is the homemade remedy of choice for diarrhea as the vegetable has binding properties.

Taro root fritters are made with raw grated taro root mixed with egg, garlic, and parsley. The tiny fritters are delicious served as appetizers. They are also often used to garnish dishes of beef or poultry.

For 20–25 fritters

Ingredients

8 ounces peeled taro root
1 large garlic clove
1 teaspoon chopped parsley
1 egg
olive oil for deep frying

Method

Grate the taro root on a fine blade, turning it into a paste. Crush the garlic with a pinch of salt in a mortar. Mix the taro root with the garlic, parsley, and beaten egg. Season with salt.

Pour the oil into a small skillet and heat on a medium heat. Drop spoonfuls of the taro root mixture into the hot oil to make the fritters. There should be enough oil to practically cover the fritters. Deep fry until golden, drain on paper towel and serve immediately.

TARO ROOT "MARIQUITAS"

Mariquitas de malanga

In the old days it was the custom in certain households to keep a tin of taro root mariquitas (ladybugs), or chicharritas as they are also called, to serve with drinks for any unexpected guests. Nowadays, these very fine slices of taro root fried till crisp are offered in certain bars to accompany the wide variety of cocktails served in Cuba.

For 4 people

Ingredients

1 white taro root, weighing about 6 ounces
olive oil for deep frying

Method

Peel the taro root and wash well.

Heat the olive oil in a skillet on a high heat. Slice the taro root extremely finely directly into the hot oil. Deep fry until golden then drain on paper towel. Dust with salt and serve.

MOJITO

The mojito and the daiquiri are the two best known cocktails in Cuba. Mojito is a delicious drink, ideal as an aperitif before embarking on a magnificent Cuban meal. The cocktail can be accompanied with some fresh pork scratchings or crunchy taro root chips, especially if you want to keep your head when the weather's very hot and thirst drives you to drink more than one.

This recipe makes up the base for the cocktail and can be kept for a long time, thus avoiding the necessity to gather fresh ingredients every time. Keeping the mixture does not spoil the flavor as the alcohol in the rum acts as a preservative. Making the basic mixture in advance means that you can quickly produce mojitos when required and also makes the preparation of large quantities of the cocktail much easier.

Ingredients

1 cup sugar
1 cup fresh lime juice
a bunch of mint
1 bottle (75 cl) 3-year-old rum

Method

To prepare the mojito base: beat the sugar, lime juice, and mint together (including the stalks) until you get a greenish liquid and the mint is completely chopped. Add the rum and beat for one more minute. This liquid can be kept in the fridge for at least a month.

To prepare a mojito: quarter fill a tall glass with the prepared liquid, add 3 ice cubes and fill the glass with sparkling water. Add a sprig of mint, if wished, stir, and serve. It doesn't matter if no mint is available, as the cocktail base is already flavored with mint.

SHRIMP BREASTS

Pechitos de camarón

Erasmo is a personality in the gastronomic world of Havana, and his restaurant La Finca is one of the best known in the city. He is an enigmatic figure whose life story is full of fantastic tales, such as the one where he was Che Guevara's cook when the revolutionaries were camped out in the mountains of the Sierra Maestra before the triumph of the Revolution in 1959. What is fact is that the shrimp pechitos and shrimp in soy sauce that he serves in his restaurant are delicious.

For 25 pieces

Ingredients

25 jumbo shrimp heads
¾ cup wheat flour
olive oil for deep frying

Method

To obtain the shrimp breast, take hold of the head and separate the outer shell that covers the head from the inner part to which the legs are attached. Keep this inner part, clean well, and cut the legs in half. Wash and dry the breasts well.

Toss the shrimp breasts in a generous amount of flour so that they are fully covered, and deep fry them in oil until golden. Drain on paper towel, sprinkle with salt, and serve immediately.

> These are delicious as an aperitif, tasting as crunchy as crackers.

Chapter 4

Soups and appetizers

BACÁN

Bacán is a dish that is made only in the region of Baracoa, the town on the north coast of the far east of the island. This region, which is extremely difficult to reach by land, was isolated from the rest of the island for a long time and has some customs that have more in common with other Caribbean islands than Cuba itself; amongst these customs is the use of coconut milk in cooking.

The region produces a great deal of fruit including the coconut and the "*guineo*," the local name for bananas. Bacán is a small pasty made with green bananas mixed with coconut milk and seasoned with garlic and lime. The pasty can be filled with pork as in this recipe, or with stewed crab or smoked meat. The pasties are cooked wrapped in banana leaves and are eaten either at lunch or with milky coffee for breakfast.

For 8 people

Ingredients

For the pork stuffing:
9 ounces lean pork meat
2 tablespoons oil
½ cup chopped onion
⅓ cup chopped green pepper
4 garlic cloves
1¾ cups peeled, seeded, and chopped tomato
1 tablespoon white wine

1 banana leaf
7 green bananas (approximately 4 ounces each)
1 teaspoon lime juice
4 garlic cloves
¼ teaspoon annatto powder or oil
7 tablespoons coconut milk (see recipe for Coquimol, page 114)

Method

For the pork stuffing: Dice the meat into ¾ inch cubes. Heat the oil in a saucepan and sauté the meat for approximately 15 minutes until golden. Add the onion, the pepper, and the garlic first crushed in a mortar. Sauté on a low heat for 3 minutes then add the tomato. Cook for 6–8 more minutes, stirring occasionally, and add the wine. Season with salt. Cover and cook for around 10 minutes on low heat until the meat is tender and swimming in a thick vegetable sauce.

For the wrapping: Cut the banana leaf into eight rectangles 7 x 10 inches, and eight 3 x 10 inches. Wash the pieces of banana leaf well and boil them in water for 1 minute so that they lose their stiffness and become malleable. Dry them well.

25

Peel the bananas by making incisions along each fruit then removing the strips of skin one by one. Grate the bananas on a fine blade, then add the lime juice, the crushed garlic, and the annatto powder combined with the coconut milk. Season with salt and pepper, and mix well. The mixture will not be very thick but it will thicken up once it has been cooked in the banana leaves.

Place two pieces of banana leaf, one of each size, on the countertop, in the shape of a cross. Place two tablespoons of the banana mixture in the middle and a line of the stewed meat on top. Fold the leaves over to form a little rectangular packet and tie like a parcel with kitchen string.

Cook the bacáns in plenty of boiling water for 30 minutes then drain.

They can be served in their wrapping or the banana leaves can be removed before serving them on a dish. Bacáns can also be eaten cold although they are not as tasty.

Annatto is a food coloring that usually contains ground annatto seeds and without which the bacán is an unappetizing gray color. In Cuba the coloring is often prepared at home by soaking the annatto seeds in a little warm oil and using this oil as a coloring.

COD CROQUETTES

Croquetas de bacalao

Croquettes have always been easy and cheap to make, and with Cuba's current economic problems they feature regularly in work canteens and in the cardboard food boxes that are distributed at special events and fiestas. These little fried mouthfuls are often made to use up leftovers and can be flavored with any small quantity of beef, poultry, ham, fish, etc. Croquettes certainly have their detractors: the Cuban comedian and writer Mongo "P." has said: "I have a friend who won't eat homemade croquettes because he knows what's in them and he won't eat those made in restaurants because he doesn't know what's in them." (*Costumbrismos Cubanos*, Ed. Si-Mar S.A., 2000. p.66)

For 6–8 people

Ingredients

10 ounces boned and desalted dried cod (see method)
3 tablespoons oil
1 cup finely chopped onion
2½ ounces butter
¾ cup wheat flour
3 cups milk
2 eggs
1½ cups breadcrumbs
olive oil for deep frying

Method

To desalt the cod, soak it in water for 24–36 hours, changing the water three or four times. Once it has been desalted, remove the skin and bones and flake the fish.

Heat the oil in a skillet on a low heat, and sweat the onion slowly for approximately 20–25 minutes until soft but not colored. Add the cod, sauté for 10 more minutes and put aside.

Melt the butter in a saucepan and add the flour. Cook for 2–3 minutes and add the milk little by little, stirring energetically until it boils, so as to obtain a smooth lump-free white sauce. Cook on a very low heat for 25 minutes, slowly stirring until the sauce has thickened considerably. It is very important that the sauce reaches the right thick consistency or the croquettes will fall apart when they are fried.

Add the cod mixture to the white sauce, cook for 10 minutes more, season with salt and pepper, then spread the mixture on a plate to a thickness of 1–1½ inches. Allow the mixture to cool for 2–3 hours.

Form the croquettes using about a tablespoon of the mixture for each one. Dip them in the beaten egg, then coat with breadcrumbs.

Heat the oil in a skillet on a high heat. Deep fry the croquettes until they are golden and drain on paper towel. Serve immediately.

> When frying the croquettes, do not put too many at a time into the skillet as that will lower the temperature of the oil and the croquettes may fall apart.

CASSAVA PASTIES WITH CHICKEN "ALCAPARRADO" FILLING

Empanadas de yuca rellenas de picadillo de pollo alcaparrado

Cassava is processed in different ways. *Catibía* is obtained by grating the cassava and squeezing out the juice that contains all the starch. This flour is used to make casabe, fritters, etc. Cassava can also be boiled and mashed into a smooth, creamy dough as in this recipe. Cassava is rich in starch and the polysaccharides that belong to the carbohydrate group. Cassava starch is often used to starch linen or cotton clothes before ironing

Alcaparrado is a mixture of raisins, olives, and capers that is often used in Cuban cooking. Nowadays each ingredient must be bought separately, whereas alcaparrado used to be sold ready mixed.

For 24–26 pasties

Ingredients

For the pastry:
1 pound cassava, washed and peeled
¼ cup wheat flour
1 tablespoon butter
1 egg yolk

For the filling:
3 tablespoons oil
¾ cup chopped onion
¾ cup chopped green pepper
6 tablespoons tomato paste
6 ounces ground cooked chicken
1 tablespoon capers
1 tablespoon pitted, chopped green olives
2 tablespoons seedless raisins
1 tablespoon dry Cuban cooking wine
1 hard-boiled egg, chopped

oil for deep frying

Method

For the pastry: Cook the cassava in plenty of boiling water for 45–50 minutes until it swells and becomes tender. Drain, and remove the hard central core. Mash the cassava by passing it through either a mincer or a sieve. Dust a countertop with flour and place the cassava paste on top. Make a hole in the center of the mixture and put in the flour, butter, egg yolk, and a pinch of salt. Knead until all the ingredients are well mixed. The mixture should not be sticky— if it sticks to your fingers, add more flour but take care, since the more flour there is in the mixture, the harder it will be.

Roll out the mixture on a floured surface to a thickness of about ¹⁄₁₀ inch. Cut out circles about 4 inches in diameter and set aside.

For the filling: Heat the oil in a skillet and add the chopped onion and pepper. Fry lightly for 2–3 minutes without allowing to brown, then add the tomato paste. Cook for another 2 minutes then add the ground chicken, capers, olives, raisins, and wine. Cook on a moderate heat for around 10 minutes then add the chopped egg. Season with salt and allow to cool.

Place a teaspoon of the chicken mixture onto half of each of the circles of cassava mixture without letting it reach the edges. Fold the dough over to form a semicircular pasty and press the edges together lightly with a fork to seal.

Deep fry the pasties in very hot oil until they are golden. Drain on paper towel and serve immediately.

These pasties are also delicious filled with cheese.

The amount of flour needed will vary according to the condition of the cassava. If too much flour is used, the pastry will be quite hard, but if too little is used, the pasties will soak up too much oil when frying. When cooked, the pastry should be light and very tender.

AVOCADO AND SHRIMP SALAD

Ensalada de aguacate y camarones

The shellfish that are to be found along the Cuban coastline include lobster, conch, blue and stone crabs, scallops, and clams. Of them all, shrimp are probably the favorites. There are two main species of shrimp in Cuba, the white shrimp (*Litopenaeus schmitti*) and the pink shrimp (*Farfantepenaeus notialis*). Shrimp are used in salads, stews, in sauces, or simply fried in batter.

For 4 people

Ingredients

1 pound jumbo shrimp
14 ounces avocados, peeled and seeded
2 tablespoons lime juice
3 tablespoons virgin olive oil
1 tablespoon finely chopped onion
1 teaspoon chopped fresh cilantro

Method

Remove the heads of the shrimp and cook the tails in salted, boiling water for 3–4 minutes. Drain, allow to cool, and peel. Take care to remove the dorsal thread from the shrimp.

Cut the avocado into thick pieces. Put into a salad bowl, and mix with the lime juice, salt, and a tablespoon of oil.

Dress the shrimp with the rest of the oil and the chopped onion. Add to the avocado and mix carefully. Sprinkle with the cilantro and serve.

You can use the discarded heads to make Shrimp Breasts (page 23).

CHICKEN, PAPAYA, AND PINEAPPLE SALAD

Ensalada de pollo, papaya y piña

In Cuba, salads often mix fruit and vegetables with beef, poultry, seafood, and sometimes even pasta. These salads are always refreshing in the intense heat.

For 4 people

Ingredients

4 ounces bacon
2 tablespoons oil
12 ounces papaya, cut into pieces approximately 1 inch square
2 tablespoons lime juice
6 ounces pineapple, cut into small triangles
4 ounces grilled chicken, flaked
1 teaspoon finely chopped scallion

For the mayonnaise:
2 egg yolks
½ cup oil
2 teaspoons lime juice

> Use a firm fleshed papaya that is not too ripe.

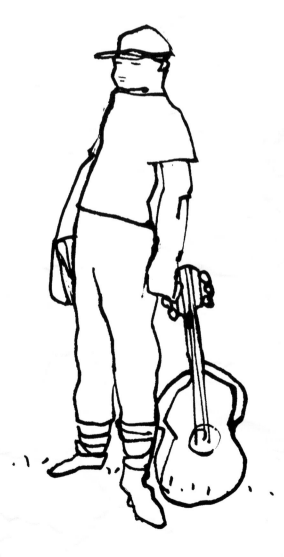

Method

Cut the bacon into tiny pieces. Heat the oil in a skillet and fry the bacon pieces until crispy. Drain on paper towel.

Put the papaya pieces into a salad bowl, add the lime juice, and mix carefully. Add the pineapple and flaked chicken.

For the mayonnaise: Beat the egg yolks and add the oil little by little, beating all the time, until thick. Season with salt and pepper, and the lime juice. Mix the mayonnaise into the other ingredients and sprinkle the bacon and chopped scallion on top.

COD FRITTERS

Frituras de bacalao

Like so many other ingredients, salt cod was imported into Cuba. Cod was part of the slaves' basic diet during colonial times being a cheap and easily conserved protein. In the sugar mills, one person was charged with distributing the salt cod ration and such was the importance of the job that the expression "he who cuts the cod" is still used to indicate a person with power.

There are many dishes made with salt cod, including cod with yam, with corn, and *aporreado de bacalao*, etc. What was slave food in the past is now a rare and expensive product much missed by Cubans.

For 12–15 fritters

Ingredients

8 ounces flaked and desalted salt cod (see method)
2 eggs
¼ cup wheat flour
2 tablespoons very finely chopped onion
1 garlic clove
1 tablespoon chopped parsley
oil for deep frying

> You can also use leftover cooked salt cod for this dish, although raw is better.
>
> The addition of parsley was only introduced in the nineteenth century.

Method

To desalt the cod, soak it in cold water for 24–36 hours, changing the water several times. Once desalted, remove the skin and bones, flake the fish and weigh out the required amount.

Beat the eggs with a fork and mix into the flour until it is smooth and lump-free. Add the chopped onion, the garlic crushed in a mortar, the chopped parsley, and the cod. Season with salt.

Heat the oil in a skillet and drop in spoonfuls of the mixture to make the fritters. Deep fry until golden on both sides and drain on paper towel. Serve immediately while still hot.

OKRA STEW WITH PLANTAIN DUMPLINGS

Quimbombo con bolitas de platano

Okra is a vegetable that came to Cuba with slavery. I have heard that the slaves hid the seeds in their loincloths, although this may be a myth. Whatever the truth of the matter, this dish is of pure African origin in both its main elements: the okra and the plantain. As is the method of cooking the plantain and adding it as dumplings to the stew.

Okra is as popular with all Cubans today as it was with the slaves and is prepared in many different ways: as salad, with chicken, in soups, with shellfish, etc.

For 4–6 people

Ingredients

5 speckled plantains, about 8 ounces each
4 tablespoons oil
12 ounces lean pork, cut into 1 inch cubes
2/3 cup chopped onion
2 garlic cloves
2/3 cup chopped green pepper
1 cup peeled, seeded, chopped tomato
2 tablespoons tomato paste
1/4 tablespoon ground cumin
1/4 tablespoon dried oregano
1/4 tablespoon paprika
1 3/4 pounds okra, cleaned and sliced into 1/2 inch circles
4 cups veal or chicken broth

Method

Wash the plantains, remove the ends, and cut each into three pieces. Cook them in boiling water in their skin for 30–40 minutes until tender. Drain, peel, and mash them well with a mortar, fork or sieve to obtain a purée. Form the purée into balls the size of large marbles and set aside.

Heat the oil in a pan on a high heat and fry the meat for around 15–20 minutes until golden. Reduce the heat and add the onion, crushed garlic, and pepper. Sauté for 5–6 minutes then add the tomato and tomato paste. Stir for a few more minutes then add the cumin, oregano, and paprika. Finally add the okra, cook for 10–12 minutes, then add the broth. Season with salt and cook gently for 15–20 minutes. Add the plantain dumplings 5 minutes before serving. The stew should not be dry, and should have plenty of creamy juices.

To judge whether okra is fresh, break off the end with your fingers—it should separate easily. If it feels hard or difficult to cut, the okra is no good.

When cleaning okra you should top and tail them, as the extremities are harder than the rest.

When cooked, okra gives off a viscous substance. This can be removed by adding something acidic, such as lemon or vinegar. In this recipe, the acid in the tomatoes normally gets rid of the viscosity but if it is not enough, add lemon juice or vinegar.

BLACK BEAN STEW

Potaje de frijoles negros

Bean stews are daily fare at the Cuban table, which may seem surprising in view of the climate. They are usually served with the plain boiled rice that is also eaten daily. Beans used for stews in Cuba include white beans, kidney beans, black-eyed beans, dried peas, and chickpeas. Black bean stew is one of the most popular and is full of flavor even if cooked without any animal protein.

There are probably almost as many recipes for bean stews as there are Cubans. Each recipe has its secret: some add vinegar, others white wine, sometimes cilantro is used, and so on. Some of these recipes are classics, such as "bean stew in the style of the Menocal sugar mills" (Menocal was one of the presidents of Cuba) that include tomatoes or "sleeping" beans, which make the broth of the stew very thick.

For 4 people

Ingredients

2 cups black beans
8 cups water
1 bay leaf

For the sofrito:
6 tablespoons olive oil
3 ounces streaked pork lard, cut into 4 pieces
2 leaves fresh oregano or ½ teaspoon dried oregano
4 medium garlic cloves
½ cup finely chopped onion
½ small green pepper, cut into strips
½ teaspoon ground cumin
1 teaspoon sugar
2 tablespoons vinegar

Method

If the beans are not tender, soak for 3 hours but no longer or they will lose color. Boil the beans in the water with the bay leaf for approximately 1½ hours, or until they soften.

For the sofrito: Heat 5 tablespoons of the oil in a pan and fry the lard pieces until golden. In a mortar, crush the oregano with the garlic into a paste. Add the garlic mixture to the pan and fry for 1 minute. Add the onion and pepper, stir-fry for a further 3–4 minutes then finally add the cumin. Add 2 tablespoons of beans to the mixture, let them cook for some minutes, then mash them with a wooden pestle so that they will thicken the stew later.

Add the sofrito to the pan of softened beans. Season with salt, the teaspoon of sugar, the vinegar, and the remaining tablespoon of olive oil. Cook for 15–20 minutes on a medium heat and serve.

Bean stew is tastier if prepared the day before.

If you use a pressure cooker to soften the beans, they will need less time and less water but they are more inclined to fall apart.

The best guarantee for achieving a good black bean stew is to use very fresh, tender beans that thicken the stew when cooked and melt in the mouth like butter.

AVOCADO SOUP

Sopa de aguacate

Cold soups have never been a regular dish in Cuba, where the norm is to see a Cuban tucking into a steaming plate of bean stew with rice at the height of August when temperatures are in the nineties. However, habits are changing.

The avocado season in Cuba lasts throughout the hottest period of the summer and into the autumn. This is a refreshing and light soup for the season. It can also be seasoned with fresh grated ginger to give it a more distinctive flavor. In Cuba, ginger is usually obtained from herbalists rather than food shops. These herbalists sell all kinds of plants and herbs, both for the Afro-Cuban Santería religious rituals and for herbal medical remedies.

For 4 people

Ingredients

12 ounces avocados, peeled
3 cups beef or chicken broth
1 teaspoon mustard
2 teaspoons lime juice

Method

Mix all the ingredients in a blender until creamy. Season with salt and pepper. If the mixture is too thick, add more broth.

Serve the soup very cold. If you like, sprinkle with plantain chips (see page 16).

GREEN PLANTAIN SOUP

Sopa de platano verde

The plantain is an essential element in the Cuban diet. It is used in its different grades of ripeness according to the dish to be prepared. Plantains are green when the outer peel is green and the flesh is very firm; speckled when the peel has green and yellow patches and the pulp is softer; mature when the peel is completely yellow and the flesh is soft and less white.

This tasty and simple soup could easily provide a light supper on its own in any Cuban household and it is often made for children.

For 4 people

Ingredients

2 green plantains, about 8 ounces each
2 cups beef broth
4 tablespoons fresh lime juice
2 garlic cloves

Method

Peel the plantains by making incisions along the length of the skin before removing. Cut the plantain into 1–1 ½ inch pieces and put them in a pan with the broth. Cook for 30–40 minutes until the plantains are tender.

Blend the cooked plantains with the broth, the lime juice, and the garlic until it is creamy. Sieve the soup to get rid of the black seeds at the core of the plantain, season with salt, and serve hot with a slice of lime or lemon.

If you cook the plantain straight after peeling there is no need to rub it with lemon and it will not discolor the soup.

STEWED TAMAL

Tamal en cazuela

The *agromercados* or *mercados agropecuarios* or, simply, "agros," are the farmers' markets in urban areas, established in 1994 to improve the distribution of agricultural products. The markets offer mainly fruit, salad leaves, cereals such as rice and corn, vegetables, and pork and mutton. There is often a stall that sells cornmeal ready milled or fresh corn flour. Though logically this should be sold by volume, it is in fact sold by weight and the meal needs to be used quickly or it ferments and becomes bitter.

Stewed tamal is a thick purée of corn seasoned with pork and a sofrito. Sofrito, a mixture of onion, green pepper, and tomatoes sautéed in oil to which other spices such as cumin, oregano, and cilantro are often added, is the basic seasoning for many Cuban dishes.

For 6 people

Ingredients

8 ounces lean pork, cut into 1 inch cubes
2 tablespoons sour orange juice
4 ½ cups freshly ground cornmeal
2 tablespoons oil
¾ cup very finely chopped onion
4 garlic cloves
½ small green pepper, cut into strips
1 cup peeled, seeded, and chopped tomato

Method

Marinate the pork in the sour orange juice for 2–3 hours.

Mix the cornmeal with about 1 ½ cups of water, and sieve to get rid of the kernel skins. You can prepare ground corn yourself at home by grating the fresh kernels directly from the cob or by grinding loose kernels in a blender.

On a high heat, fry the meat for 7–10 minutes in the oil until golden. Reduce heat and add the onion, crushed garlic, and pepper. Cook for a few more minutes then add the tomato. Stir-fry for a further 4–5 minutes then raise the heat and add 1 cup of water. When it starts to boil, add the sieved cornmeal and cook, stirring constantly, until it reaches boiling point again. Reduce the heat and allow to cook slowly for 30–40 minutes, stirring occasionally, until you have a thick creamy purée. Season with salt. If the mixture is too thick, add water. Pour into a bowl and serve at once. As it cools it becomes hard and loses its creamy texture.

The amount of water you will need will vary with the quality of the cornmeal. If it is rich in starch the mixture will thicken more than you expect and will need more water. If you buy the meal ready ground, water has often already been added and you will need less.

TAMALES WRAPPED IN LEAVES

Tamal en hojas

Although this dish is similar in flavor to stewed tamal, the appearance and texture are quite different. In this recipe, the cornmeal seasoned with stewed meat is wrapped in corn leaves, forming little packets that are boiled in water until they harden. When the leaves are opened, they reveal a flavorsome cornmeal pasty. They are a favorite lunch dish for many Cubans on beach picnics and in certain regions of the country where they are also known as "tallullos," although when they have that name, they are usually wrapped in banana leaves.

For 8–10 pieces

Ingredients

10 corncobs
3 tablespoons water
8 ounces lean pork
2 tablespoons oil
2/3 cup chopped onion
1/3 cup chopped green pepper
4 garlic cloves
1 3/4 cup peeled, seeded, and chopped tomato
1 tablespoon dry Cuban cooking wine

Method

Grate the corn kernels from the cob, or grind them if they are loose in a food processor or blender until you have a paste. Mix with the water and pass through a sieve until you have a creamy mixture.

Cut the meat into 1/2 inch pieces. Heat the oil in a skillet and fry the meat until very golden for approximately 15 minutes. Add the onion, pepper, and crushed garlic. Sauté on a low heat for 3 minutes, then add the tomato. Stir-fry for 6–8 more minutes, stirring occasionally, and add the wine. Cover and cook on a low heat for around 10 minutes until the meat is tender. Add the corn paste and stir. Season with salt and pepper.

Wash and dry the corn leaves. Form a cross with four leaves by placing two leaves in each direction. Put a good spoonful of the mixture into the centre of each cross taking care that it does not spill over the edge. Fold over into a secure rectangular packet and tie like a parcel.

Boil the tamales in water for an hour and drain. They can be eaten either hot or cold.

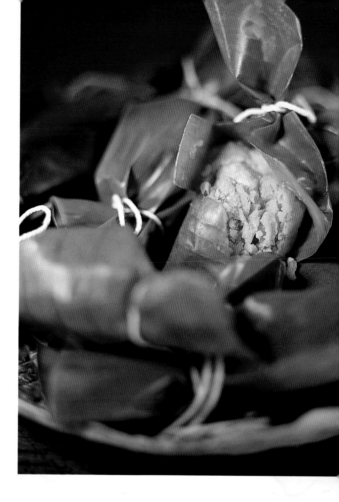

Chapter 5

Main dishes

BERTA'S MINCEMEAT

Picadillo al estilo de Berta

Berta María Rodríguez García, a descendent of African slaves, was born in Camagüey. At thirteen years old she started work as a cook in a family home, later moving to Havana to work for other households. After a long life full of pleasures and pains, Berta is now nearly eighty and still cooking for her own family with the same skill and zest that she learned in childhood. Her stews encapsulate the sensitivity of a noble and dignified person who has devoted her life to her work and family. Her word is law when it comes to the correct way of creating and seasoning traditional Creole dishes. This recipe for mincemeat, a classic of Creole cuisine, follows Berta's dictates. The dish is called "a la Habanera" if olives and raisins are added.

For 4 people

Ingredients

2 garlic cloves
1 leaf fresh oregano (or ½ teaspoon dried oregano)
1 pound ground beef
⅓ cup finely chopped onion
2 tablespoons dry Cuban cooking wine
¼ teaspoon ground cumin
½ small green pepper, cut into ¼ inch strips
4 tablespoons olive oil
7 tablespoons tomato paste
12 pitted green olives

Method

Crush the garlic with the oregano and a pinch of salt in a mortar.

Marinate the meat for 30–45 minutes with the onion, wine, cumin, green pepper, oil, tomato paste, olives, garlic, and oregano.

Put the mixture into a skillet and cook on a medium heat for approximately 15 minutes or until the meat is tender. If it needs cooking for longer, add 2 or 3 tablespoons of broth or water, as the mince should remain slightly liquid. Adjust seasoning and serve hot.

> The fresh oregano used in Cuba is a variety with large, quite hairy leaves and a mild flavor.
>
> This dish is traditionally accompanied by white rice, black bean stew, fried eggs, and vegetables such as fried plantain.

ROAST LEG OF PORK, CREOLE STYLE

Pierna de cerdo asada a la criolla

The roast leg of pork or spit-roast piglet served with cassava in garlic sauce, green plantain tostones, and rice and beans were the typical fare of *guajiros* or country people in the old days. Nowadays it is the favorite menu for any important event and is the classic celebration food for New Year's Eve, the most important festival in Cuba since 1959 as it celebrates not only the New Year but also the Triumph of the Revolution.

The tastiest pork comes from pigs fed on *palmiche*, the fruit of the royal palm, that sprout on little branches around the trunk. In the countryside, once the branches have been stripped of fruit, they are turned into brooms.

For 10–12 people

Ingredients

1 leg of pork, weighing approximately 12 pounds

For the marinade:
1 large head of garlic (or 2 small)
3 teaspoons salt
1 teaspoon ground cumin
½ teaspoon black pepper
2 teaspoons dried oregano
1½ cups sour orange juice

Method

The leg of pork should be marinated the evening before being roasted. Remove the skin of the leg and all bones except the main bone that joins the trotter. When the skin and bones have been removed, the leg should weigh around 7½ pounds.

For the marinade: Crush the garlic in a mortar with the salt, cumin, pepper, and oregano. Add the orange juice and mix well.

Place the pork in a large dish and cover well with the marinade. Cover the dish and leave to marinate for 12–14 hours, turning the meat every now and again so as to make sure all parts absorb the marinade.

To roast the pork, heat the oven to 350° F and place the meat in an earthenware dish, keeping the marinade aside. Roast for around 5 hours, basting occasionally with the marinade. The meat should be well cooked inside and golden outside.

Once cooked, remove the leg of pork from the dish and strain the juices. Serve the pork cut into slices accompanied by its own juices.

> For the pork to be at its most flavorsome, roast slowly and for a long time.
>
> The same marinade is used in the country for spit-roast pork and suckling pig.

STUFFED PEPPERS

Pimientos rellenos

Peppers, native to tropical America, are an essential element of Cuban cooking. Apart from being a basic ingredient of the sofrito that seasons so many dishes, peppers are also roasted, used in salads, or stuffed as in this recipe. Both green and red peppers are used in Cuba, as is a small, ridged, sweet-flavored variety of bell pepper called *"cachucha"* that provides mainly seasoning or decoration.

For 4–5 people

Ingredients

For the sofrito:
6 tablespoons oil
1 ¼ cups chopped onion
6 garlic cloves
⅓ cup chopped green pepper
½ teaspoon dried oregano
¼ teaspoon ground cumin
1 cup tomato paste
6 tablespoons dry Cuban cooking wine
3 tablespoons vinegar

1 pound ground beef
3 tablespoons chopped green olives
3 tablespoons raisins
8 green peppers (around 1 pound)
¼ cup breadcrumbs
⅔ cup water
3 tablespoons dry Cuban cooking wine

Method

For the sofrito: Heat the oil in a skillet on a medium heat and stir-fry the onion, crushed garlic, and chopped pepper for 7–10 minutes without letting them brown. Add the oregano and cumin, stir, and add the tomato paste. Sauté for another 10–12 minutes, add the wine and vinegar, and cook for another 45 minutes. Season with salt and pepper.

Divide the sofrito into thirds and set two thirds aside for the sauce. Add the beef, olives, and the raisins, that have first been soaked in warm water and drained, to the remaining third of the sofrito. Season with salt and pepper and cook on a

medium heat for 15 minutes until some of the liquid has reduced.

Wash the peppers well, cut a hole around the stalk and clean all the seeds out. Fill the peppers with the mincemeat mixture and seal the opening with breadcrumbs.

Heat the reserved sofrito with the water and cooking wine in a flameproof earthenware dish large enough to take all the peppers quite snugly. Add the peppers, cover, and bake on a medium heat for around 30 minutes, turning once. Serve in the same dish.

FRIED CHICKEN, CREOLE STYLE

Pollo frito a la criolla

The secret of this dish's flavor is the garlic and lime marinade that adds something special. This tasty dish appears frequently in Cuba both in restaurants and private homes and it is rare to find it badly cooked.

For 4–6 people

Ingredients

3 ½ pound chicken
5 garlic cloves
½ cup fresh lime, lemon or sour orange juice
oil for deep frying
1 ½ cups wheat flour

Method

Joint the chicken and cut the breasts in two.

Crush the garlic in a mortar with a teaspoon of salt and add the lime juice. Marinate the chicken in this for approximately 3 hours.

Heat the oil in a skillet on a medium heat. Drain the pieces of chicken, and coat them thoroughly in flour. Fry gently for about 12–15 minutes, until golden. Drain on paper towel, dust with salt, and serve.

For the chicken to be crunchy, it is very important to coat the pieces thoroughly in the flour by pressing each piece very firmly between your hands when flouring them so that as much flour as possible will adhere to the chicken.

The chicken must fry slowly, otherwise it will be golden on the outside and raw inside.

CHICKEN "RANCHO LUNA"

Pollo "Rancho Luna"

This recipe originated in the Rancho Luna restaurant and is still served to much acclaim at one of Havana's most popular restaurants, El Aljibe, where they make a genuinely Creole meal of this by serving the chicken with white rice, "sleeping" black beans, fried green plantain, and a salad.

The secret of this chicken dish is the delicious sweet-sour sauce produced in the roasting. Very few have been able to guess the precise ingredients, which remain as closely guarded as a state secret by the restaurant. This is my version.

For 4 people

Ingredients

3 ½ pound chicken
2 tablespoons oil
1 ½ onions, sliced into rings
5 garlic cloves
1 ¾ cups sour orange juice
½ cup chicken broth
1 teaspoon cornstarch

Method

Clean the chicken well and tie for roasting. Rub with salt and the oil. Heat the oven to 350° F.

You will need a roasting dish with a rack. Scatter the onion rings on the base of the roasting dish, place the chicken on the rack, and put the dish into the oven.

Crush the garlic in a mortar with a pinch of salt and add the sour orange juice. When the roasting onion starts to brown—after about 20 minutes—baste the chicken with the garlic and orange mixture. Continue basting little by little, a spoonful at a time, during the whole cooking time of around 1–1 ½ hours.

Once the chicken is cooked, remove it and cook the juices and onion left in the roasting pan on top of the stove on a gentle heat. Add the broth and deglaze the pan. Sieve the gravy and pour into a small saucepan. Dissolve the cornstarch in cold water and add to the gravy if necessary to thicken it. Cook for 4–5 more minutes on a low heat.

Carve the chicken and serve the sauce either in a separate dish or poured over the meat.

> Don't begin basting the chicken until the onion starts to brown or the flavor of the sauce will be affected.
>
> If the sauce is thick enough there is no need to add cornstarch. There should be a lot of sauce.

MEATLOAF

Pulpetas

In Cuba, beef is normally stewed in a flavorsome sauce to mix with the rice or viandas that accompany the main dish. In this dish, ground beef is first rolled into a loaf and stuffed with boiled egg, which makes a surprise appearance when the loaf is sliced, then cooked in a rich sauce.

For 4–5 people

Ingredients

5 ounces cooked ham
½ cup milk
½ cup fresh breadcrumbs
1 onion
12 ounces ground beef
6 ounces ground pork
1 egg
2 hard-boiled eggs, peeled
4 tablespoons oil
2 garlic cloves
½ teaspoon dried oregano
⅔ cup dry Cuban cooking wine
½ cup broth
1 teaspoon vinegar

For coating the meatloaves:
1 egg
½ cup dry breadcrumbs

Method

Chop the ham very finely. Bring the milk to a boil and pour over the breadcrumbs. Allow to cool. Chop half the onion very finely and cut the other half in strips.

In a bowl, mix the ground beef and pork with the ham, chopped onion, soaked breadcrumbs, and raw egg. Season with salt and pepper. Knead the mixture well and divide into two oval-shaped loaves. Put a hard-boiled egg into the center of each and reshape carefully.

Dip the loaves first into the beaten egg, then into the dry breadcrumbs. In a deep pan or skillet, heat the oil on a high heat and fry the loaves until golden on all sides, taking care that they don't fall apart.

Remove the loaves and set aside, then add the strips of onion and the cloves of garlic to the pan. Sauté for 5–8 minutes without allowing them to brown. Add the oregano, cooking wine, and the broth. Season, and return the meatloaves to the pan. Add the vinegar. Cover and cook for 40–50 minutes on a low heat, turning the loaves once halfway through cooking.

Slice and serve hot, covered with the sauce.

CASABE ROLLS WITH DRIED BEEF

Rollitos de casabe con tasajo

Casabe is possibly the only surviving example in Cuba of indigenous cooking. It is a type of bread made with cassava that has been grated, squeezed to extract the poisonous juice containing natural cyanide, sieved, and grilled in cake-shaped pasties on iron griddles. These pasties are sold in the market wrapped in dry *yagua*. *Yagua* is the lower part of the royal palm leaf, which sticks to the trunk until it comes off the tree. Once dry and stretched, the leaves look like corrugated cardboard and can be used to make containers.

This traditional Camagüeyan dish was apparently a favorite of the writer Gertrudis Gómez de Avellaneda (1814-73). A delicious version is served in the El Morro restaurant, situated by the Morro fortress in Santiago de Cuba with a wonderful view of the sea.

For 5 people

Ingredients

5 casabe cakes
12 ounces pounded dried beef (see page 57)
3 eggs
3 tablespoons wheat flour
oil for deep frying

Method

Soak the casabe cakes gently under running cold water. This must be done with great care or the cakes may fall apart. Let them rest for some minutes.

Cut each cake into two rectangular pieces, approximately 4 x 6 inches. Place 1 ½ tablespoons of dried beef in the middle of each piece, and fold into a packet, making sure that no meat is exposed.

Beat the eggs and season with salt. Dip each packet into flour and then into the beaten egg. Deep fry in hot oil until golden, and drain on paper towel. Serve very hot with a salad.

ROPA VIEJA

Ropa vieja is a dish, like so many others in Cuba, that has its origins in Spanish tradition. As the Spanish diplomat and author Agustín de Foxá wrote: "*Los emigrantes españoles viajaban como los buzos, con atmósfera propia.*" ["The Spanish immigrants carried the very air they breathed along with them like divers."] (Various authors, *Gusta Usted? Prontuario culinario y necesario*, La Habana, 1956. p.598). However, in the wake of the long journey, this stew adapted its flavors to the tastes of a warmer climate.

For 6–8 people

Ingredients

To boil the meat:
1 onion, quartered
1 tomato
3 garlic cloves
½ teaspoon ground cumin
½ green pepper
3 pounds beef brisket

To flavor the stew:
4 tablespoons white wine
3 large garlic cloves
2 leaves fresh oregano or 1 teaspoon dried oregano
7 tablespoons oil
¾ cup finely chopped onion
½ medium green pepper, cut into julienne strips
1 teaspoon ground cumin
½ cup tomato paste

Method

To boil the meat: Put the quartered onion, together with the tomato, garlic, cumin, pepper, meat, and a pinch of salt into a pan. Add water until it covers the ingredients. Place on a high heat and when it starts to boil, skim the surface carefully. Reduce the heat and cook gently for approximately 2 hours, until the meat is tender. Allow to cool before removing the meat and sieving the broth.

The next stage is to stew the meat. Flake the meat into threads, removing any skin or fat that may remain. Place into a bowl and add the white wine and some salt.

Crush the garlic in a mortar with the oregano. Heat the oil in a skillet and fry the garlic and oregano. Add the onion and sauté for 2–3 more minutes. Add the strips of pepper, fry for a few minutes more, and add the cumin and the tomato paste. Fry for a further minute then add the meat. Mix well, add about 1½ cups of the meat broth, cook for another 10 minutes. The ropa vieja should not be too dry but have some sauce.

Serve this stew with congrí rice and fried plantains.

51

YAM PIE

Tambor de ñame

This dish is made with typically Creole seasoned mincemeat covered with a yam purée. The classic recipes for the dish use potato or plantain purée but yam purée has a fine, light texture that enhances the stew. Some claim that the yam is native to Africa and others that it comes from the Americas. What is certain is that yams now grow abundantly in the tropical regions of both continents and stay fresh a long time after being harvested. Yams must never be eaten raw as they are toxic until cooked. In Cuba, yams are usually served as a side vegetable, covered in a garlic and oil sauce.

For 4 people

Ingredients

For the base:
1 leaf fresh oregano or ½ teaspoon dried oregano
2 garlic cloves
1 pound ground beef
½ cup chopped onion
2 tablespoons dry Cuban cooking wine
½ teaspoon ground cumin
½ small green pepper, cut into julienne strips
4 tablespoons oil
7 tablespoons tomato paste
4 tablespoons pitted chopped green olives
2 tablespoons capers
4 tablespoons raisins

For the yam purée:
1 ¼ pound yams, peeled
¾ cup milk
2 ounces butter

1 teaspoon fresh chopped parsley

Method

For the base: Crush the oregano with the cloves of garlic and a pinch of salt in a mortar. Marinate the meat in a bowl with the onion, wine, cumin, green pepper, oil, tomato paste, olives, capers, raisins, and garlic and oregano paste for 30–45 minutes.

Put the meat and marinade into a skillet and cook on a medium heat for approximately 15 minutes, or until the meat is tender. If you need to cook it for longer, add 2 or 3 tablespoons of broth or water as the mixture should not be dry. Season with salt. Spread the meat mixture out in a baking dish measuring approximately 8 x 6 inches to a depth of around 1 inch.

For the yam purée: Cut the yam into pieces and cover with water in a saucepan. Boil with the lid on for around 30–40 minutes. Drain and mash. Boil the milk with 4 tablespoons of the butter. Mix the yam purée with the milk and butter, and season with salt and pepper. Spread the purée on top of the meat, taking care not to mix them. Dot the dish with the rest of the butter and cook at 400˚F for 30 minutes. Remove from the oven, sprinkle with the chopped parsley, and serve.

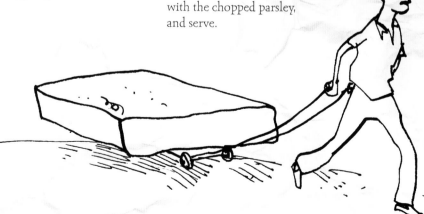

FRIED DRIED BEEF

Tasajo en pencas

In colonial times, the port of Havana was the last stop for all the ships sailing from the Americas before the final crossing of the Atlantic en route for Spain. It was here that ships stocked up with provisions for the long crossing. One of the foodstuffs taken on board was dried beef or biltong, an easily conserved form of protein. That is why the production of dried beef developed in Cuba.

Fried dried beef is simple to prepare but delicious, especially when accompanied by Glazed Sweet Potatoes (page 89).

For 6 people

Ingredients

2 pounds dried beef
6 tablespoons oil
4 garlic cloves

Method

The evening before cooking, soak the dried beef for around 8–10 hours to desalt it.

Cover with water in a pan and cook for 2–2 ½ hours until tender. Drain and remove any remaining traces of skin or gristle. Depending on the quality of the dried beef, you will be left with between 1 ¼ and 1 ½ pounds of clean beef. Cut into strips approximately 1 inch thick and tenderize by beating gently with a wooden pestle.

Heat the oil in a skillet and add the strips of dried beef and the crushed garlic. Sauté for 3–4 minutes and serve. When frying, do not allow the beef to brown, or it will become too tough. It should simply turn pinkish.

AJIACO

Cubans often refer to their own culture metaphorically as an "ajiaco," as it is formed from elements brought by all the different people who came to the island.

Ajiaco is a rich stew, incorporating various green vegetables, tubers, and corn, as well as a variety of different meats. There are probably as many versions of this dish as there are regions or cities in Cuba. There are ajiacos from Bayamo, Puerto Principe (nowadays Camagüey), Trinidad, etc. Each regional version varies slightly as to which meats are used and how the corn is incorporated, whether as flour dumplings, slices of corncob, etc.

For 10–12 people

Ingredients

12 ounces dried beef
1 pound beef brisket
1 pound pork ribs
1 pound loin of pork
8 ounces white taro root, peeled
6 ounces yellow taro root, peeled
12 ounces cassava, cleaned and peeled
9 ounces potatoes, cleaned and peeled
9 ounces yam
2 green plantains, each about 8 ounces
2 speckled plantains, each about 8 ounces
8 ounces squash
3 corncobs
1 pound sweet potato, cleaned
10–12 lime wedges

continued on page 56

For the sofrito:
6 tablespoons oil
5 large garlic garlic cloves
1 ¼ cups very finely chopped onion
⅓ cup chopped green pepper
½ teaspoon ground cumin
2 ½ cups peeled, seeded, and diced tomato

Method

The evening before, soak the dried beef in water to desalt it. Change the water two or three times.

Put all the meat into a pan, cover with 20 cups of water and cook on a high heat until it starts to boil. Skim the surface to remove impurities. Season with salt and cook gently for 1 ½ hours.

Meanwhile, prepare the vegetables. Cut the taro root, cassava, potatoes, and yam into large pieces approximately 2 inches square. Put the pieces aside in cold water. Score the plantains in strips lengthwise with the point of a sharp knife and remove peel. Rub the green plantain with lemon juice to stop them discoloring. Cut each plantain into four pieces.

Divide the cleaned squash into two. Cut the corncobs into 1 inch thick slices. (The sweet potatoes must be peeled at the very moment of being added to the pan as they go black as soon as they are peeled. Once peeled, cut them into thick pieces like the taro root.)

For the sofrito: Heat the oil in a skillet on a gentle heat and fry the crushed garlic, onion, and pepper for 4–5 minutes. Add the cumin and tomato. Cook for 15–20 minutes and then set aside.

Once the meat has cooked, add the vegetables to the pan, little by little, starting with those that take the longest to cook. Add the corn first, then the taro root, the yam, and the cassava. After 20 minutes, add the green plantain and the squash. After another 20 minutes, add the sweet potato, the potato, and the speckled plantain. Add the sofrito and cook for 40–50 minutes. Season with salt. When the vegetables are cooked, remove the meat from the pan, clean it and remove the bones from the ribs, cut it into pieces and put back into the pan. To thicken the sauce, remove the pieces of squash, mash them, and return them to the pan.

The ajiaco should be a slightly thick broth with the pieces of vegetable still intact and not fallen to pieces. It is served in soup bowls with lime wedges on the side.

Traditionally, the corn can be incorporated into the ajiaco in three ways: as slices cut from the cob, as fresh corn flour or as corn flour dumplings. Sometimes two different methods are used at once, for example slices of corncob and fresh corn flour or ground corn are both added.

This is primarily a vegetable dish in which the meat is mainly used as a flavoring. Even so it is eaten as a main dish.

It is important not to use too much taro root as it imparts too distinctive a flavor to the dish.

POUNDED DRIED BEEF

Aporreado de tasajo

In colonial times, dried beef along with salt cod were the basic sources of protein with which slaves were fed. Both products were cheap on the international market and easy to preserve, bearing in mind that ice did not reach Cuba until 1806. Although a certain amount of dried beef was produced in Cuba, the majority was imported. The home-produced and imported varieties were distinct from each other, and the imported variety was dubbed "*brujo*"

(wizard) because it appeared to increase in quantity when cooked, as though by magic. Nowadays, like salt cod, dried beef is an expensive product available to few but greatly appreciated.

For 3–4 people

Ingredients

1 pound dried beef
7 tablespoons oil
1 ¼ cups finely chopped onion
½ green pepper, cut into strips
1 tablespoon chopped fresh parsley
3 garlic cloves
3 cups ripe tomato, peeled, seeded, and diced.

Method

The evening before cooking, wash the dried beef and soak for 10–12 hours to desalt it.

Cover the beef in water and cook for 2–2 ½ hours, or until tender. Drain and allow to cool. Cut into slices and remove any traces of skin and gristle. Tenderize the beef by pounding with a wooden pestle and flake into threads.

Heat the oil in a skillet on a medium heat and stir-fry the onion, pepper, parsley, and crushed garlic for 4–5 minutes. Add the tomato and cook for 20–30 minutes until the tomato is mushy. Add the meat. Mix well and cook for another 15–20 minutes. Adjust seasoning. The stew should be quite liquid.

Serve accompanied by fried casabe (cassava flour cakes).

SUSANA'S RICE WITH GREEN PLANTAIN

Arroz con plátano verde al estilo de Susana

Susana Hernández is a woman with a particular sensitivity for anything that has unique beauty or a touch of "Cubanness." She was born and spent her childhood in the Sierra Maestra, a very rural and mountainous region in the province of Santiago. She still remembers being sent out to buy a chicken by her mother and scolded if she came back with one that was too thin. Life and work brought Susana to Havana but she still recreates for her friends and neighbors the special dishes her mother taught her in the countryside, like this unusual dish of rice with green plantains.

For 4 people

Ingredients

1 pound lean pork (leg or shoulder)
4 tablespoons oil
½ teaspoon ground cumin
1 cup peeled, seeded, and diced tomato
1 teaspoon vinegar
1 cup diced green pepper
1 cup finely chopped onion
3 tablespoons chopped scallion
5 garlic cloves, chopped
1½ cups Valencian rice
8 ounces green plantain, peeled (see note) and diced small
1 leaf serrated cilantro
3 cups fresh grapefruit juice

For dressing 1:
2 heaped tablespoons chopped serrated cilantro
1 tablespoon virgin olive oil
1 teaspoon cider or balsamic vinegar

For dressing 2:
2 heaped tablespoons chopped scallion
1 tablespoon virgin olive oil
1 tablespoon cider or balsamic vinegar

Once it has been peeled, green plantain should be kept in water with lemon juice or it will go black. To peel, make incisions every inch along its length with a sharp knife and remove the skin.

The Cuban grapefruit is not as acidic as others. If using a more acid grapefruit, dilute with a little broth or orange juice, making sure the correct proportion of liquid is maintained.

The ratio of liquid to rice given here is for round-grained Valencian rice. If other types of rice are used, the amount of liquid (grapefruit juice) should be adjusted accordingly.

Method

Cut the meat into cubes approximately 1 inch square. In a heavy pan, heat the oil on a medium heat and add the meat, cumin, and a pinch of salt, and fry for 20–25 minutes until the meat is well browned. Add the tomato, sauté for 1 or 2 minutes and add the teaspoon of vinegar. Add the pepper, onion, 2 tablespoons of scallion, and the garlic. Raise the heat and sauté for 4–5 minutes stirring occasionally and taking care that it does not stick to the pan. Finally add the rice, plantain, and cilantro leaf; sauté for a few more minutes then

add the grapefruit juice. Season with salt and cook for approximately 15–20 minutes until the rice is tender and all the liquid has been absorbed.

When it is cooked, allow to rest for 5 minutes then place in an earthenware dish and sprinkle

the remaining chopped scallion on top. Serve with one of the two dressings.

For the dressings: In separate bowls, mix the ingredients for each dressing and season with a pinch of salt.

CHICKEN AND RICE "A LA CHORRERA"
Arroz con pollo a la Chorrera

Rice and chicken prepared in various different ways have always been daily staples in the Cuban diet and remain so today. Chicken and rice "a la Chorrera" originated in la Chorrera del Vedado hotel, where a nineteenth-century chef, Monsieur Petit, created the famous dish. Originally, Monsieur Petit flavored it with sherry but over time beer rather than wine has become the classic ingredient.

For 6 people

Ingredients

For the marinade:
12 garlic cloves
1 teaspoon dried oregano or 1 leaf fresh
$\frac{1}{2}$ teaspoon ground cumin
2 tablespoons chopped onion
3 tablespoons fresh lime juice

$1\frac{1}{2}$ pounds jointed chicken
$\frac{1}{4}$ cup oil
$\frac{3}{4}$ cup chopped onion
1 green pepper, cut into thin strips
5 tablespoons tomato paste
$\frac{1}{2}$ teaspoon annatto powder or oil
6 cups chicken broth
1 bay leaf
3 cups Valencian rice
$1\frac{1}{2}$ cups beer
1 cup cooked green peas
2 small grilled red peppers, cut into strips

Method

For the marinade: Crush the garlic, oregano, and cumin with some salt in a mortar. Add the onion and lime juice.

Place the chicken pieces in a dish and season with salt. Add the marinade, mix well, and leave for at least an hour.

Drain the chicken pieces and keep the remaining marinade. Heat the oil in a heavy pan on a high heat. Fry the chicken until golden then remove from pan. Reduce the heat and add the onion, green pepper, and the remaining marinade. Sauté for 5–6 minutes until the onion is transparent, then add the tomato paste and the annatto powder. Cook for another 5–6 minutes then add the chicken pieces, the broth, and the bay leaf. Season with salt, cover, and cook gently for 25 minutes. Raise the heat, add the rice and cook for 15 minutes. When the rice starts to dry out and is almost cooked, add the beer and peas and cook for another 5–10 minutes, until the rice is cooked but still fairly liquid.

Place in an earthenware dish, garnish with strips of red pepper, and serve immediately before the rice dries too much.

The rice for this dish must be a round-grained variety, such as the Spanish Valencian or Italian Arborio. If another type of rice is used, the amount of liquid and cooking time required will be different.

In this dish the rice should not be completely dry but fairly soupy.

TUNA WITH SUGAR CANE AND COCONUT GLAZE

Atun a la caña de azucar con glaseado de coco

Paladares are restaurants in private houses where the owners serve food in their own dining room. These restaurants became established when tourism began to peak around 1995 as a means to remedy a difficult economic situation. *Paladares* need to be licensed by the authorities, and licenses are granted only if certain regulations are met, among which are that no more than 12 people can be served at a time and no beef can be offered.

The name "*Paladares*" came from a Brazilian television soap that was hugely popular in Cuba, in which the heroine, faced with ruin, began selling sandwiches in the street and ended up as the rich owner of a restaurant chain called "La Paladar." *Paladares* have grown into excellent restaurants where you can sample everything from tasty home cooking to creative, sophisticated dishes that may indicate new directions in Cuban cuisine.

One of the best known *Paladares* in Havana is La Guarida, which is situated in the building where the Oscar-nominated film *Strawberry and Chocolate* was shot. Enrique and Ode Núñez, the owners, tired of opening their doors to so many visitors curious to see the film's location, decided to turn it into a *Paladar* and offer meals. This recipe is one of the stars on the restaurant's menu and reflects the new direction of culinary interest in Cuba.

For 1 person

Ingredients

For the coconut glaze:
1 1/3 cups shredded fresh coconut
1 star anise
1/2 cup soy sauce
2 tablespoons 7-year-old rum

For the salad:
1 ounce peeled lobster tail
1 ounce peeled shrimp
1 teaspoon olive oil
1 tablespoon diced green pepper
1 tablespoon diced red pepper
1 tablespoon peeled, seeded, and diced cucumber
2 teaspoons chopped scallion
1 tablespoon finely chopped red onion
1 1/2 teaspoons virgin olive oil
1/2 teaspoon fresh lime juice
1/2 teaspoon chopped fresh cilantro

For the fish:
2 pieces of fresh tuna cut into 2 inch squares (about 4 ounces)
2 pieces sugar cane, 3 inches long and 1/4 inch thick
1 tablespoon olive oil

Method

For the coconut glaze: In a pan, cook the shredded coconut, star anise, soy sauce, and rum until the mixture is reduced by half. Remove the star anise, combine the mixture in a blender, sieve it, and set aside.

For the salad: Rub the lobster and shrimp with the olive oil and sauté in a skillet on a medium heat for 2–3 minutes. Once they have cooled, cut into small strips. In a bowl, mix the shellfish with the green and red peppers, cucumber, scallion, and red onion. Make a dressing by combining the virgin olive oil, lime juice, and cilantro with salt and pepper. Mix well with the salad. Set aside.

For the fish: Cut a hole in the center of one side of each piece of tuna. Insert a piece of sugar cane into each hole making sure that half the cane sticks out. Heat the oil in a skillet and fry the tuna pieces until golden on all sides. Brush the tuna with the coconut glaze and sauté for a few more minutes. Season with salt before serving.

Place the tuna on a dish with the sugar cane sticking out on one side. Pour the rest of the glaze from the skillet over the fish and serve the shellfish salad on the side.

STEAK CASSEROLE

Bistec en cazuela

A simple and savory stew to make the best of less tender joints of meat. The secret, as with so many Cuban dishes, lies in the marinade.

For 5–6 people

Ingredients

2½ pounds top rump, cut into 5 or 6 steaks
½ cup fresh sour orange juice
½ cup oil
2 onions, cut into strips
4 garlic cloves
1 teaspoon dried oregano
¾ cup beef broth

Method

Marinate the steaks in the sour orange juice, seasoned with salt and pepper, for 45 minutes. Heat the oil in a deep skillet on a high heat and brown the marinated steaks. Remove the meat and set aside and reduce the heat. Add the onion and crushed garlic to the pan and sauté for 8–10 minutes without allowing to brown. Add the oregano and return the steaks to the pan. Add the remaining marinade and the broth. Raise the heat until the stew begins to boil then reduce again and cook gently for 30 minutes, until the meat is very tender and the sauce thick.

To serve, arrange the steaks in a dish, place the strips of onion on top and pour the sauce over them. The sauce should be thick and not too plentiful.

LAMB WITH VEGETABLES

Carnero con vegetales

This is a simple, savory country dish. Cubans enjoy stews and broths with which they can soak their rice. If the lamb is somewhat tough, an infallible trick is to marinate the meat in fresh papaya juice the evening before cooking. This household tip has a scientific explanation, as papaya contains an enzyme that helps to break down proteins.

For 10 people

Ingredients

1 leg of lamb, approximately 3 ½ pounds
4 garlic cloves
4 tablespoons fresh lime juice
⅔ cup peeled, seeded, and diced tomato
3 cups peeled, sliced carrots
4 onions, cut into strips
1 cup tomato paste
1 cup dry Cuban cooking wine
2 pounds peeled potatoes, cut into 1 inch cubes
1 cup peas

For the sofrito:
8 tablespoons oil
⅓ cup chopped onion
⅔ cup chopped green pepper

Method

Remove the bone from the leg of lamb and clean it well of all remaining bits of skin and fat. Cut the meat into 1 inch cubes. You should be left with around 2 pounds of clean meat.

Marinate the meat for an hour with the crushed garlic mixed with the lime juice and some salt.

For the sofrito: Heat the oil in a large pan on a medium heat and sauté the onion and pepper for 8–10 minutes.

Raise the heat, add the lamb, and fry for approximately 15 minutes until lightly golden. Add the diced tomato, carrot, onion, tomato paste and wine. Season with salt and pepper and after 15 minutes, add the potatoes, mix well, cover the pan and cook on a low heat for another 40 minutes. Add the peas, adjust the seasoning, and cook for another 10 minutes. The stew should be juicy but not watery. The vegetables should be soft but not falling apart.

GROUPER "A LO PRINCIPEÑO"

Cherna a lo Principeño

This recipe appeared for the first time in the cookery book *Manual del Cocinero Criollo* (The Creole Cook's Handbook), published in 1856. The dish was most probably named after the city of Puerto Príncipe, now Camagüey, although curiously the town is not a port.

Cuba's coastal waters are full of exquisite and varied fish among which the favorites are grouper, red snapper, and hogfish. This dish can equally well be made with red snapper.

For 4 people

Ingredients

1 pound grouper fillets
2 tablespoons fresh lime juice
6 tablespoons olive oil
¾ cup chopped onion
2 garlic cloves
¾ cup peeled, seeded, and diced tomato
2 tablespoons capers
1 tablespoon chopped parsley

Method

Cut the fish fillets into pieces approximately 2 x 2½ inches and marinate in the lime juice and some salt for 10 minutes on each side. The fillets should be no thicker than ½ inch.

Heat 4 tablespoons of the olive oil in a skillet on a low heat. Add the onion and crushed garlic. Sauté for approximately 6 minutes until the onion is soft but not browned. Raise the heat slightly, add the tomato and stir-fry for 10–15 minutes, until all the tomato liquid has evaporated. Season with salt and keep on a low heat.

Heat the rest of the oil in a skillet on a high heat and fry the fish fillets until golden on both sides. Do not overcook the fish or it will be dry. Arrange the fish fillets in a serving dish, spoon the tomato sauce over them, and sprinkle with capers and chopped parsley before serving.

PLANTAIN CROQUETTES WITH DRIED BEEF FILLING

Croquetas de platano rellenas de aporreado de tasajo

Dried beef and plantains were basic ingredients in the slave diet, but since the slaves were the ones who cooked for their masters, they transposed the flavors and stews that they liked to the masters' table. Among the dishes they produced must have been these delicious and elaborate plantain croquettes filled with dried beef.

For about 7 croquettes

Ingredients

3 speckled plantains (around 8 ounces each)
1 tablespoon milk
3 egg yolks
1 tablespoon butter
2 tablespoons wheat flour
5 ounces pounded dried beef (see page 57)

For coating and frying:
2 eggs
½ cup breadcrumbs
olive oil for deep frying

Method

Cook the plantains without peeling them in boiling water for 30 minutes until they are soft.

Test with a fork. Peel the plantains while they are hot by scoring along their length with a sharp knife, then removing the skin in strips. Cut them in half lengthwise and remove the core with a teaspoon. Mash the plantains.

Put the mashed plantains, milk, egg yolks, butter, and flour into a bowl. Season with salt and mix well by hand until the mixture is a homogenous mass that does not stick to the sides of the bowl. If it seems too sticky, add some more flour.

On a countertop, roll the mixture into a long thick roll and divide into about seven pieces. Form each piece into a ball and make a hole in the center with your thumb. Fill the hole with the dried beef and fold and seal.

When all the croquettes are ready, dip them first in beaten egg, then in breadcrumbs. Deep fry the croquettes in a skillet full of very hot oil until they are golden. Drain on paper towel and serve immediately.

JOSÉ'S CEVICHE

Crudo de pescado al estilo de José

This is a typical sailor's dish and, according to my friend José who has been a sailor since his youth and is the son of a fisherman, it is not worth preparing if you do not have olive oil.

King mackerel or wahoo are both excellent fish to use but the dish is also delicious with red snapper. It is very good served with Cucumber Salad (page 91).

For 4 people

Ingredients

1 pound king mackerel or wahoo (with no skin or bones)
2 tablespoons chopped onion
12 tablespoons lime juice
4 tablespoons virgin olive oil
1 teaspoon chopped parsley

Method

Cut the fish into ¼ inch cubes and place in a bowl. Add the onion and lime juice. Mix well and leave in the fridge to marinate for at least 3 hours. The lime juice should completely cover the fish.

To serve, drain off the lime juice, season the fish with salt and pepper, arrange on a dish, and drizzle the olive oil over it. Finally, sprinkle with chopped parsley.

> Chopped cilantro can be used instead of parsley.
>
> While it is marinating the fish will keep for several days in the refrigerator as the lime preserves it.

EMBOZADO HABANERO

This is a very old Cuban dish that first appeared in a nineteenth-century publication on Creole cooking. The word *"embozado"* means something hidden or camouflaged by a cloak. In this case what is hidden is the delicious highly seasoned filling, rolled into the fillets and braised.

For 6–8 people

Ingredients

For the stuffing:
11 ounces lean pork, chopped
5 ounces ham, chopped
½ teaspoon ground cinnamon
2 ground cloves
1 teaspoon dried oregano
1 tablespoon vinegar

1¾ pounds beef steak (14–15 pieces)
9 ounces fresh pineapple, diced
½ cup oil
2 onions, cut in strips
2 tablespoons vinegar
1 cup dry Cuban cooking wine
½ cup beef broth

Method

For the stuffing: In a bowl, mix the pork, ham, cinnamon, cloves, oregano, and vinegar. Add salt and pepper and leave for an hour to marinate.

Lay the steaks out on a surface. They should be no thicker than ¼ inch. Divide the stuffing between the steaks, placing a roll in the middle of each. Place a row of pineapple pieces on top of the stuffing. Roll the steaks around the stuffing, so that the stuffing is enclosed, and tie with kitchen string so that they do not come open while cooking. Season with salt on the outside.

Heat the oil in a pan and fry the rolls of steak until brown. Put the steaks to one side, add the onion to the pan and sauté gently for 5 minutes until golden. Put the steaks back in the pan along with the vinegar, wine, and broth. Raise the heat and when it starts to boil, reduce, cover, and cook for approximately 30 minutes until the meat is tender. The sauce should reduce considerably and stay quite thick. If necessary, remove the steaks and reduce the sauce until it reaches the right consistency.

Remove the string, arrange the steaks on a serving dish, and pour the sauce over them.

LOBSTER "ENCHILADO"

Enchilado de langosta

No day's fishing in Cuban waters is complete without a succulent lunch of lobster "enchilado" served with white rice and some mojitos or daiquiris. In pure Hemingway style, after catching some wahoo or tuna, the lobsters destined for lunch, and, with luck, some coveted marlin, the perfect end to a day's fishing is to stop the boat and have a swim while preparing the lobster for lunch.

The name "enchilado" comes from the hot spice used in the cooking. It should be added with a very light touch, as Cubans do not eat highly spiced foods.

For 6 people

Ingredients

4 lobster tails (around 8 ounces each)
1 tablespoon fresh lime juice
8 tablespoons oil
1 ¼ cups chopped onion
½ cup chopped green pepper
4 garlic cloves
1 ¾ cups peeled, seeded, and diced tomato
4 tablespoons tomato paste
½ teaspoon sweet paprika
1 cup white wine
½ cup fish broth
1 bay leaf
½ teaspoon cayenne or chili pepper
1 tablespoon chopped parsley

Method

Remove the lobster tail shells. Make a small incision in the back of each tail to remove the intestine. Cut the lobster tails into pieces about 1 ½ inches thick. Marinate the lobster pieces in the lime juice with some salt for 15–25 minutes.

Heat the oil in a skillet on a high heat, sauté the lobster, then remove and place in a pan. Reduce the heat and add the onion, pepper, and crushed garlic to the skillet. Stir-fry without allowing to brown for 15 minutes. Add the diced tomato, the tomato paste, and the paprika. Cook for a further 10–12 minutes and add the wine and fish broth. Cook gently for 5 minutes, then add the bay leaf and cayenne pepper. Season with salt.

Pour this sauce into the pan with the lobster and cook on a gentle heat for 10–12 minutes, until the lobster is tender but not dry. Serve sprinkled with chopped parsley.

Shrimp can also be used for this recipe.

RED SNAPPER "A LA SANTA BÁRBARA"

Filetes de pargo a la Santa Bárbara

In the region of Baracoa in Guantánamo province, dishes incorporating coconut milk are called "a la Santa Bárbara." In Afro-Cuban religious syncretism, Chango is the *orisha*, or god, of war, fire, lightning, virility, and music. The Roman Catholic equivalent is Saint Barbara, and this deity is one of the most powerful and revered in Santería. Since coconut is a ritual food offering for the Santería or syncretic deities, it is very likely that dishes cooked with coconut milk were named for Saint Barbara for religious reasons.

For 4 people

Ingredients

⅓ cup flour
2 eggs
⅔ cup shredded fresh coconut
1 tablespoon chopped scallion
1 tablespoon chopped parsley
1 pound red snapper fillets
oil for deep frying

For the sauce:
½ cup finely chopped onion
1 ounce butter
⅔ cup white wine
1¼ cups coconut milk (see recipe for Coquimol, page 114)
1 teaspoon wheat flour
1 pinch annatto powder or 1 teaspoon annatto oil

Method

For the sauce: Sauté the onion in two thirds of the butter for 3–4 minutes on a low heat without allowing it to brown. Add the wine and coconut milk and cook until the liquid is reduced by half. In a separate pan, fry the teaspoon of flour in the rest of the butter. Add this to the first mixture to thicken the sauce, add the annatto, and cook for 5–7 minutes more on a low heat until all taste of flour has gone. Season with salt and pepper. Purée the sauce and set aside in a saucepan. The sauce should be light and not too thick.

Place the flour in a shallow bowl and the beaten eggs in another. In a third bowl, place the shredded coconut mixed with the chopped scallion and parsley. Season the fish fillets with salt, cover each fillet first with the flour, then the egg, and finally the coconut mixture. Heat the oil in a skillet on a high heat and deep fry the fish until golden. Drain the fish on paper towel.

Serve the fish immediately with the very hot sauce handed separately.

> It is common to add annatto to dishes using coconut milk in order to give them a yellowish or orange color. Annatto is a natural colorant and adds no flavor.

LOBSTER "A LA HABANERA"

Langosta a la habanera

Although lobster is found in seas around the world, the Cuban lobster that is exported to various places is considered particularly fine and flavorsome. If there is one lobster expert in Cuba it is chef Gilberto Smith Duquesne, who has spent much of his life promoting Cuban lobster around the world and cooking it for many illustrious people. He has even published a book entitled *King Lobster*, describing his own ways of cooking the crustacean. This is a version of one of his creations.

For 4 people

Ingredients

2 small pineapples, approximately 1¼ pounds each
2 lobster tails, around 8 ounces each
1 tablespoon fresh lime juice
2 tablespoons butter
1 tablespoon rum
1 tablespoon chopped scallion

For the sauce:
4 ounces butter
5 egg yolks

Method

Cut the pineapples into equal halves. Cut the flesh carefully out of the pineapples and set aside. Clean the insides of the pineapple halves carefully and set them aside, skin side uppermost so that the juice can drain away. Remove the hard center of the fruit and cut the rest of the pineapple flesh into small pieces.

Remove the shell from the lobster tails. Make an incision into the back of each and remove the intestine. Cut the lobster into 1 inch pieces and marinate in the lime juice with some salt for 10 minutes.

Melt the butter in a skillet without allowing it to burn, and sauté the pieces of lobster for 2–3 minutes. Season with salt, add the rum, and flambé. Cook for 2–3 minutes more, then remove, and set the lobster aside on a plate.

For the sauce: Melt the butter in a pan until it is liquid. Skim and clarify the melted butter. Beat the egg yolks in a bowl set in a pan of hot water until they go pale. Carry on beating the yolks and at the same time slowly adding the melted butter until it becomes a creamy sauce. The sauce should be quite thick or it will dilute too much when it is mixed with the lobster and pineapple. Season the sauce with salt and pepper.

Mix the lobster carefully with the chopped pineapple and all but 2 tablespoons of the sauce and fill the pineapple halves with the mixture. Decorate with the reserved sauce, sprinkle with chopped scallion, and serve. This dish should be served lukewarm.

PORK "CONFIT"

Masitas de puerco

Sour orange is an essential ingredient in Cuban cooking; it has the virtue of being sour without being bitter. The juice of the orange is vital for sauces and marinades as well as for making fresh orange drinks. The skin of the orange is used in a dessert. The sour orange has other uses—the pulp is used to clean tiles and restore them to brilliance! In times of scarcity in Cuba, such as during the "special period" that covered approximately the decade from 1990–2000, Cubans become very ingenious at finding new uses for available resources. If they clean tiles with sour orange juice, they are just as likely to clean silver with toothpaste.

The secret of making delicious pork "confit" is to marinate the meat in sour orange and allow it to cook gently in the melted pork fat until it is very tender.

For 4–5 people

Ingredients

2½ pounds lean leg of pork
¼ cup sour orange juice
7 ounces pork fat

Method

Cut the meat into cubes approximately 2 inches square and marinate for an hour in the sour orange juice.

Heat the pork fat in a pan and add the pork pieces. Season with salt. Once the mixture begins to boil, reduce the heat, and cook for around 1½ hours. All the cooking liquid should evaporate leaving only the fat. The pieces of pork should soak in the fat and be very tender. Remove from the heat and drain the fat. Serve very hot, accompanied by black bean stew, white rice, cassava with garlic sauce, and plantain fritters.

This is a typical country dish and is usually accompanied by the side dishes indicated, but it is also very good with Stewed Tamal (page 38).

75

RED SNAPPER WITH CAPERS

Pargo con alcaparras

This recipe incorporates almonds and capers, both common ingredients in Cuban cooking although, like many other ingredients, they are not indigenous and were imported by Spanish immigrants.

For 6–8 people

Ingredients

1 ½ pounds red snapper fillets
2 tablespoons fresh lime juice
2 tablespoons oil
1 tablespoon chopped parsley

For the sauce:
6 tablespoons oil
1 ¼ cups chopped onion
2 tablespoons chopped parsley
½ cup toasted almonds
2 tablespoons capers
1 ¼ cups fish broth

Method

Cut the red snapper fillets into pieces approximately 3 inches long and marinate them in the lime juice with some salt for 10 minutes on each side.

For the sauce: Heat the oil in a skillet on a low heat and add the onion and parsley. Sauté for around 6 minutes, until the onion is soft but not browned. Grind the almonds and capers separately in a mortar and add to the pan. Cook for 2 minutes and add the broth. Raise the heat and once the mixture begins to boil, reduce it again and cook gently for 10 minutes. Season with salt.

Heat the oil in a skillet on a high heat, fry the fish fillets quickly until golden on each side and pour the sauce over them. When it begins to boil, cook for 1–2 more minutes then remove from the heat. Serve in an earthenware dish sprinkled with chopped parsley.

CELIE'S CHICKEN AND CORN PIE

Pastelón de pollo y maíz al estilo de Celie

Although Celie left her homeland over forty years ago never to return, she still remembers nostalgically many of the traditional Cuban recipes served in her home, and she recreates them for her family and friends in exile. This dish is one of them.

The *pastelón* is a traditional dish from the area of Camagüey and consists of a pastry filled with meat or poultry stew and vegetables cooked in the oven. In this version, the pastry is slightly spongy and only covers the stew on top, which results in a juicier dish.

For 6–8 people

Ingredients

6 tablespoons oil
3½ pounds jointed chicken (1½ birds)
1¼ cups chopped onion
2 garlic cloves
6 tablespoons tomato paste
⅔ cup dry Cuban cooking wine
⅔ cup chicken broth
9 ounces cooked corn
9 ounces cooked green peas

For the pastry:
9 ounces butter
6 eggs, separated
1 tablespoon sugar
a pinch of salt
2 cups wheat flour

Method

Heat the oil in a pan on a high heat and cook the chicken pieces, seasoned with salt, until golden. Set aside. Reduce the heat and sauté the onion and crushed garlic for 4 minutes without allowing it to brown. Add the tomato paste and cook for 8–10

minutes more. Put the chicken pieces back into the pan along with the wine and broth. Raise the heat until it boils, then reduce and cook covered for 40–45 minutes, until the chicken is tender. Allow to cool.

Remove the chicken from the pan and skin and bone the pieces. Mix the chicken back with the sauce, and add the corn and peas. Adjust seasoning with salt.

For the pastry: Melt the butter and mix with the egg yolks, sugar, and salt. Add the flour and mix well. Finally, add the egg whites beaten into peaks and fold in carefully with a spatula.

Put the chicken stew into an oven dish measuring approximately 12 x 10 inches. Spoon the pastry mix over the stew and cook in an oven preheated to 400° F for 50–60 minutes, until the pastry is golden and well cooked.

FISH IN ESCABECHE

Pescado en escabeche

Escabeche is a traditional Spanish recipe that is very popular
in Cuba and is a very practical way of preserving fish.
For this dish to be completely successful, it is vital
that olive oil and wine vinegar should be used
and that they are in a 50:50 proportion. There
are various versions of this recipe: in some the
battered fish is fried first; others add olives
and/or capers; others cooked carrots, beans, or
peppers. This simple version is one that I think is
both delicious and healthy.

POR LA PATRIA LA VIDA

For 6–8 people

Ingredients

1 cup olive oil
2 onions, cut into strips
8 garlic cloves
1 cup white wine
1 cup wine vinegar
1 bay leaf
20 peppercorns
2¼ pounds fresh tuna
in slices 1 inch thick

Method

Heat the oil in a pan on a gentle heat and sauté the onion and whole garlic cloves for 10–12 minutes until they are soft but not brown. Add the wine, vinegar, bay leaf, and peppercorns, and season with salt. Add the slices of fish and raise the heat until it comes to a boil. The liquid should cover the fish. Reduce the heat and cook gently for 15 minutes until the fish is cooked. Skim the liquid of impurities while it is cooking.

Arrange the fish in a china bowl and pour the sauce over it until it is completely covered. Leave to settle for 2 days before eating. Serve cold, sprinkled with chopped onion, and accompanied with a fresh green salad.

Fish in escabeche can be kept in the refrigerator for around 25 days. It must always be covered in the sauce and always kept in a china dish not metal, which can react with the vinegar.

> **Although any fish from the tuna family is fine for this dish, it is considered tastiest when tuna or king mackerel are used.**

Chapter 6

Side dishes

CABBAGE STEW

Aporreado de col

Nowadays, no self-respecting Cuban will leave home without carrying the indispensable "just in case" *jaba* in their bag. The *jaba* is just a bag with handles, often a plastic supermarket one, and I believe the word "*jaba*" comes from the English "handbag." This item, simple to acquire and highly valued in Cuba, is essential to the daily search for food. For example, if you are walking down the street and see a passer-by selling cheap cabbages or the first mangoes of the season, you have your *jaba* at the ready to take them home. Equally, if there is food left over at a restaurant meal or event, you can quickly gather it into your *jaba* for the following day.

This dish, the cabbage for which has likely been brought home in a *jaba*, is a tasty stew seasoned with a typically Creole sofrito, flavored with cumin, oregano, paprika, and parsley.

For 4 people

Ingredients

8 tablespoons oil
9 ounces smoked loin of pork, cut into small pieces
1¼ cups chopped onion
1 green pepper, cut into strips
6 garlic cloves
1⅓ cups peeled, seeded, and diced tomato
1 teaspoon dried oregano
¼ teaspoon ground cumin
¼ teaspoon sweet paprika
⅔ cup tomato paste
1¾ pounds cabbage, cut into strips
1 teaspoon sugar
4 tablespoons dry Cuban cooking wine
4 tablespoons chopped parsley

Method

Heat the oil on a high heat in a pan and fry the pork until browned. Add the onion, pepper, and crushed garlic. Fry lightly for 5–8 minutes without allowing to brown.

Add the diced tomatoes, sauté for 5 more minutes, then add the oregano, cumin, and paprika. Mix together well and add the tomato paste. Cook gently for 5 more minutes then add the cabbage, sugar, and wine. Season with salt, stir, and cook on a medium heat, covered, for 15 minutes until the cabbage is tender. Add the chopped parsley just before serving. Serve very hot as an accompaniment to a meat or poultry dish.

RICE WITH VEGETABLES

Arroz con vegetales

In 1990, the fall of the Berlin Wall and the loss of Soviet Union subsidies brought a period of great hardship to Cuba when the population was deprived of many basic necessities. During this time, officially dubbed the "special period," many foodstuffs were in short supply. Apparently, unscrupulous individuals traded in pizzas made with melted condoms instead of cheese and in "steak" made of old rags marinated in lime juice.

Emma, a great friend and cook, told me that in her house they added whatever spices and seasonings they could find to the rice to vary the flavor. With typical Cuban humor, they baptized the dish "rice with special effects" as an allusion to the "special period." This rice with vegetables is a recipe of Emma's with some of the added refinements of more prosperous times.

For 6–8 people

Ingredients

3 ounces carrot, diced
4 ounces green beans, cut into 1 inch pieces
6 ounces chayote, peeled and cut into ½ inch pieces
½ cup oil
1¼ cups chopped onion
3 garlic cloves
¾ cup chopped green pepper
1 cup peeled, seeded, and diced tomato
3 tablespoons tomato paste
⅓ cup raisins
6 ounces peeled squash, cut into ½ inch pieces
4 ounces cooked corn kernels
1½ cups Valencian rice
⅔ cup dry Cuban cooking wine
4 ounces cooked green peas

Method

Put the carrot, beans, chayote, and a pinch of salt into a pan. Add 4 cups of water, bring to a boil, and cook for approximately 15 minutes until the vegetables are tender. Remove the vegetables and keep the broth simmering gently.

Heat the oil in a large, heavy skillet on a medium heat. Add the onion, garlic, and pepper and sweat until tender but not brown. Add the tomato and tomato paste and cook for 10 more minutes. Raise the heat and add the cooked vegetables, raisins, squash, and corn. Sauté for 3–4 more minutes then add the rice. Fry for another 3 minutes then add 2⅓ cups of the vegetable broth and the wine. The volume of the liquid should be twice the volume of the rice. Season with salt and cook for around 20 minutes, until the rice is cooked and all the liquid is absorbed. Add the peas 5 minutes before the end. Allow the rice to rest for 5 minutes, then serve in an earthenware dish.

If the green beans are very tender there is no need to cook them first: they can be added raw at the same time as the squash.

Spanish rice is known as Valencian rice in Cuba and has always been a favorite for rice dishes, although other types of rice are also used. If using a different variety, it might be necessary to adjust the amount of liquid.

CONGRÍ RICE

Arroz congrí

Although rice cooked with beans is native to the whole Caribbean, congrí is so typically Cuban that it has even given rise to the expression "more Cuban than congrí." Congrí is served frequently both at festivities and at the daily table. It can be prepared with both black and kidney beans and has different names in different parts of the island, where it is variously known as congrí, Moorish rice, or Moors and Christians. These different names are the source of much lively argument among Cubans, many insisting that congrí is made with kidney beans and Moorish rice with black beans, while others say that the type of bean has nothing to do with the nomenclature.

Apparently the French colonists who fled to Cuba from Haiti during the slave rebellion brought the word "congrí" with them: in Haiti, beans were known as "congo" and rice was "riz." According to the Cuban anthropologist Fernando Ortiz, during the decade 1868–78 the dish was known as "volunteers and firefighters," as the volunteer soldiers were white and the firefighters black.

For 6 people

Ingredients

1 cup black beans
4 ounces streaked pork lard, diced
6 tablespoons oil
3 garlic cloves
2 leaves fresh oregano or 1 teaspoon dried
²/₃ cup finely chopped onion
½ small green pepper, cut into strips
2½ cups Creole rice
½ teaspoon ground cumin

Method

Cook the beans in a pan with 6 cups of water for approximately 1½ hours until they are tender. The amount of cooking liquid remaining should be the same or slightly more than the volume of rice to be used.

Fry the lard in a pan in the oil until golden. Crush the garlic and oregano in a mortar and add to the pan. Fry gently for 1 minute and add the onion. Sauté for another 5 minutes and add the pepper. Fry for a few more minutes, then add the rice and cumin. Season with salt and mix all the ingredients together. Add the beans in their cooking liquid to the rice. Cover and cook on a low heat for approximately 15–20 minutes, until the rice is cooked and has absorbed all the liquid. Allow to rest for a few minutes then serve.

If the black beans are tender, they will not need to be soaked before cooking. If they are hard, soak them for 2–3 hours, but no more or they will discolor.

Creole or round-grained Spanish rice can be used for this dish. If the Spanish rice is used, increase the volume of liquid to twice that of the rice.

AVOCADO AND PINEAPPLE SALAD

Ensalada de aguacate y piña

At the beginning of the 1990s, when the economic hardship that led to the "special period" was declared, people who were lucky enough to have a patio or garden in urban areas uprooted their ornamental plants in favor of fruit trees to help in the hard task of feeding the family. The avocado tree was a favorite as it grows very easily. It is a native of Central America and the season in Cuba is between June and September. Those avocados—caprices of nature—that are harvested out of season are known as "sneaky avocados."

In Cuba, it is customary to put all the dishes that are going to make up the meal on the table at once. Among them there is always a salad that is especially refreshing and welcome during the time of most intense heat.

For 4–6 people

Ingredients

2–3 avocados
2 cups fresh pineapple chunks
4 tablespoons virgin olive oil
2 tablespoons cider vinegar
1 tablespoon chopped scallion

Method

Cut the avocados in half. Remove the pit and prick the flesh with a fork without piercing the skin. Distribute the pineapple chunks between the avocado halves.

Mix the oil and vinegar to prepare the dressing. Season with salt and pepper. Spoon the dressing over the avocado halves, sprinkle with chopped scallion and serve an avocado half to each person.

This salad can also use pineapple halves instead of avocado. For this version, you need 2 or 3 small pineapples cut in half lengthwise. Remove the flesh and chop. Dice the avocado, mix with the pineapple chunks and dressing and fill the pineapple halves with the mixture. Sprinkle with the chopped scallion and serve one half to each person.

For an impressive lunch or dinner with exotic visual effect, this salad can be served as an appetizer in pineapple halves on a table decorated with arrangements of a mixture of flowers and areca leaves. The areca *(Chrysalidocarpus lutescens)* is a palm originating in Madagascar but very common in Cuba.

GLAZED SWEET POTATOES

Boniatos glaseados

The Cuban sweet potato is white fleshed. It is eaten a great deal as it is easy to grow and cheap and easy to buy. It is usually served boiled with a garlic sauce or fried, and is also used to make desserts such as doughnuts or boniatillo. Sweet potato is a classic accompaniment to dried beef, and this sweet–sour version goes hand in hand with Fried Dried Beef (page 55) and also with roast turkey.

For 6 people

Ingredients

1 ¼ pounds peeled sweet potatoes
a few drops of fresh lime juice
¼ cup brown sugar
½ teaspoon ground cinnamon
2 tablespoons butter
2 tablespoons dry Cuban cooking wine

Method

Boil the sweet potatoes in water with salt and the lime juice for approximately 30–40 minutes until tender. Drain and cut into ½ inch thick slices.

Arrange the slices in an ovenproof dish and sprinkle with sugar and cinnamon. Dot each slice with butter and sprinkle with the wine. Bake for 15–20 minutes in an oven preheated to 350° F. Serve immediately.

> The sweet potatoes should be peeled under running water and placed immediately in a pan full of water to avoid them going black.

BLACK BEAN AND PEPPER SALAD

Ensalada de frijoles negros y pimiento

This tasty salad uses two ingredients native to America, black beans and peppers. If it is necessary to soak the beans because they are somewhat hard, it is best to use the same water to cook them in so as to avoid discoloration.

For 4 people

Ingredients

1 ¾ cups black beans
1 tablespoon olive oil
1 bay leaf

For the dressing:
1 ¼ pounds red bell peppers
4 tablespoons virgin olive oil
1 tablespoon sherry vinegar
½ cup finely chopped onion
1 tablespoon chopped parsley

Method

Wash the beans and put into a pan with 8 cups of water. Soak for 2–3 hours, if necessary. Add the oil and bay leaf and cook on a medium heat for approximately 1 ½ hours until cooked. Drain, allow to cool, and place in a salad bowl.

Roast the peppers in the oven or toast on a fork on the burner flame until the skin blackens and peels away from the flesh.

Carefully remove the skin and wash the peppers. Remove the seeds and white parts and cut into ¼ inch wide strips.

Once the beans are completely cold, add the oil and vinegar, the onion, and the peppers. Season with salt and mix well. Sprinkle the parsley on top and serve.

> It is not a good idea to cook the beans in a pressure cooker as they tend to disintegrate.
>
> Mix the onion into the beans just before serving as otherwise it tends to go black.

90

CUCUMBER SALAD

Ensalada de pepino

Cucumbers in Cuba are very aromatic and refreshing, as well as having the advantage of being available all year round. This salad is the perfect accompaniment to ceviche (see page 68).

For 4–6 people

Ingredients

2 pounds cucumbers
⅓ cup cream cheese
5 tablespoons virgin olive oil
2 tablespoons chopped scallion

Method

Peel the cucumbers and cut in half lengthwise. Remove the seeds and cut each half into pieces ½ inch thick. Put the pieces into a salad bowl.

For the dressing, mash the cheese with a fork and add the oil and chopped scallion. Season with salt and pepper and mix well. The mixture should remain somewhat lumpy. Mix with the cucumber and serve.

BRAISED EGGPLANT

Fritada de berenjenas

Curiously, the eggplant belongs to the same family as the potato and is widely grown in the Caribbean. This eggplant stew, seasoned with a Creole-style sofrito of onion, garlic, and tomato, is a tasty side dish. Eggplants are also often fried sliced and covered with breadcrumbs in Cuba.

For 4–6 people

Ingredients

½ cup oil
1¼ cups chopped onion
2 garlic cloves
1 pound eggplant, peeled and cut into ½ inch dice
2 cups peeled, seeded, and diced tomato
1 tablespoon chopped parsley

Method

Heat the oil in a pan on a gentle heat, and add the onion and crushed garlic. Fry gently for approximately 8 minutes until the onion is soft but not brown. Slightly increase the heat and add the eggplant. Fry for 10 more minutes and add the tomato. Cook for 15–20 minutes more, stirring occasionally, until the eggplant is tender and the liquid has evaporated. Season with salt and serve very hot, sprinkled with the chopped parsley.

> The tomatoes should be very ripe but firm. If they are acid, add a teaspoon of sugar.
>
> If the eggplant taste bitter, soak them in salt and water for 30 minutes after they have been cut. Drain and dry well before cooking.

CORN FRITTERS
Frituras de maíz

Corn is a cereal native to America and was the staple food for the indigenous people. It is still a common ingredient in Cuban cookery nowadays, processed in different ways and served in many varied dishes.

Corn fritters are simple and tasty and can be served as an appetizer or as an accompaniment to meat and poultry. Some recipes include beaten egg, but if the corn is fresh and juicy it is not necessary. The most delicious corn fritters I have ever tasted were those prepared by a woman tending a roadside stall near Santiago de Cuba. Her utensils consisted of a grater, a slotted spoon, a skillet on a wood fire, a bowl, and a plate for the fritters. Her ingredients comprised a bottle of oil and a field of ripe corn from which she took the cobs for her fritters.

For 8–10 fritters

Ingredients

7 corncobs (or 1 pound kernels)
1 tablespoon chopped scallion
oil for deep frying

Method

Grate the corn from the cob on a thick grater blade or remove all the kernels and put them in the food mixer to obtain a thick, slightly lumpy paste. Mix the crushed corn with the scallion and season with salt.

Heat the oil in a skillet on a high heat. Drop tablespoonfuls of the mixture into the pan and squash them gently with the slotted spoon so that they are around ½ inch thick. Deep fry on both sides until golden, drain on paper towel and serve.

> These corn fritters are delicious as an accompaniment to meat, poultry or fish. If you make the fritters smaller, they can be served as a tasty snack with an aperitif.
>
> It is best to use a nonstick skillet to avoid the mixture sticking.

GREEN PLANTAIN FUFÚ

Fufú de platano verde

During the colonial period, plantains were one of the slaves' favorite foods. On certain large plantations, the slaves were given small pieces of land called "*conucos*" for growing food for their own consumption, where they planted bananas, taro root, corn, etc. to supplement their diet. They were also allowed to sell the surplus and many bought their freedom with this revenue.

Fufú was the name given to certain dishes in which the main ingredient is a vegetable cooked and then puréed and seasoned in various ways. There is fufú of taro root, of plantain, and of yam. The name "fufú" apparently comes from the English "food-food" during the times of the first slave trade treaty.

For 4-6 people

Ingredients

4 ounces streaked pork lard
13 ounces lean pork
2 tablespoons oil
4 green plantains (around 8 ounces each)
6 garlic cloves

Method

Remove any skin from the pork lard and cut into 1 inch pieces. Cut the lean pork into pieces of the same size.

Heat the oil in a pan on a medium heat, add the pork and lard and season with salt. Fry until the meat is very brown, stirring occasionally, for around 30–40 minutes. The streaked pork should reduce considerably and release its fat.

Wash the plantains, cut off the ends, and slice each into three pieces. Cook the plantains in their skins in a covered pan in boiling water for 50–60 minutes. Drain and peel them. Purée the plantains in a mortar or by mashing with a fork.

Pour a little of the pork fat into a small pan and fry the crushed garlic. Add the garlic to the original pan together with the plantain purée. Mix the plantain well with the meat and garlic, cook for another 7–10 minutes, season with salt, and serve hot. The purée should be very thick and smooth, interspersed with the chunks of meat and fat.

This very traditional dish is served as an accompaniment to pork and chicken.

SWEETCORN STEW

Guiso de maiz tierno

Corn, or maize, was the staple for the island's aboriginals who apparently called it "*maisí*" or "*majisí*." This stew is similar to others on the American continent from those countries where corn is commonly eaten.

For 4 people

Ingredients

3 tablespoons oil
9 ounces loin of pork, cut into 1 inch cubes
1 cup very finely chopped onion
2 garlic cloves
½ green pepper, cut into strips
2 cups peeled, seeded, and diced tomato
4 cups fresh corn kernels
6 ounces squash, peeled and seeded
2 cups beef broth
4 threads of saffron
1 teaspoon chopped parsley

Method

Heat the oil in a pan and fry the meat until golden. Add the onion, crushed garlic, and pepper, sauté for 5 minutes and add the tomato. Cook for 15–20 minutes more until the tomato softens.

Add the corn, the squash cut into four pieces, the broth, and the saffron, and season with salt. Increase the heat and bring to a boil, then lower heat and cook for 20–30 minutes, until the corn is tender.

Remove the pieces of squash, mash them, then return the mash to the pan to thicken the broth. Cook for 10 more minutes and serve in an earthenware dish sprinkled with chopped parsley.

TEMPTATION PLANTAINS

Platanos en tentacion

As the musician Alberto Falla says: "In the country, the plantain fields have been used for purposes far removed from the plantain harvest. And closer to more earthy pleasures…" (*El Libro del sabor*, Ediciones Unión, La Habana, 1999. p.63) The same point is made by the country song "Bartolo's plantain field."

I came from Cocosolo
Because I want to dance the guaracha
Here in our friend Bartolo's plantain field.

Girl, we'll have some fun,
Look, I'm all alone
here in our friend Bartolo's plantain field.

Yo vengo de Cocosolo
porque quiero guarachar
aqui en el platanal
de nuestro amigo Bartolo

Muchacha, vamos a gozar,
mira que me encuentro solo
aqui en el platanal,
de nuestro amigo Bartolo

Temptation plantains, the name of which is as suggestive as Bartolo's plantain field, could easily be assumed to be a dessert but in Cuba the dish is served as an accompaniment to meat and poultry. It is especially delicious with roast pork.

For 4 people

Ingredients

4 mature plantains (6 ounces each)
2 tablespoons butter
2 tablespoons brown sugar
3 tablespoons dry Cuban cooking wine or rum

Method

Peel the plantains (see page 100). Melt the butter in a skillet on a medium heat. Fry the plantains for about 5 minutes until golden on both sides, reduce the heat, and sprinkle the sugar over the plantains. Turn the plantains so as to spread the sugar well and add the wine or rum. Cover the pan and cook on a gentle heat for approximately 20 minutes until they are tender inside and the sauce has caramelized. Turn the plantains over once during cooking. Serve hot.

The plantains should be very mature with yellow skins.

If the plantains are very thick they can be cut in half lengthwise.

99

PLANTAIN "TOSTONES"

Tostones de platano

In Cuba, a group of vegetables including cassava, taro root, sweet potato, yam, potatoes, squash, and plantains are known as "viandas." These vegetables, cooked in various ways, are served daily as an accompaniment to protein dishes and are also used as a basis for desserts. It is a rare Cuban home that does not have a well-stocked *viandero*, from which the person in charge of the cooking selects the viandas to be prepared. Some of these *vianderos* are exquisite objects made of wood or ornate wrought iron while the most modern of them are plastic.

Tostones are one of the many ways of cooking plantain and are very commonly eaten in Cuban homes.

For 6 people

Ingredients

3 green plantains
olive oil for deep frying

Method

Peel the plantains by making longitudinal incisions along the skin with a sharp knife and removing the strips. Cut the plantains into slices 1 ½ inches thick. Arrange the slices in a skillet and cover with oil. Cook them on a gentle heat until tender but not golden.

Remove the slices of plantain from the oil, drain, and flatten them with the palm of the hand or the bottom of a glass until they are about ½ inch thick.

Put ½ cup of water and a tablespoon of salt into a bowl. Wet the slices of plantain in the water then deep fry them in very hot oil until golden. Drain on paper towel. The tostones should be crisp on the outside and tender on the inside. Serve immediately.

In the old days, tostones were fried in pork fat instead of oil, and in some places this is still the case. Nowadays, because of the price of olive oil, sunflower oil is often used instead.

During the first cooking, the tostones should be boiled or simmered in the oil rather than fried.

CASSAVA IN GARLIC SAUCE
Yuca al mojo de ajo

It is common to use the leftovers of cassava in garlic sauce to make fried cassava, cutting the cassava into chunks and frying in plenty of oil until golden. The cassava should be fresh and recently harvested if it is to soften and open up when cooked. If cassava is not going to be eaten as soon as it is bought, it is best to peel and freeze it. A good guide as to the quality of the cassava is how easy it is to peel. If the skin comes off easily, the vegetable is much more likely to be tender.

This delicious garlic sauce is used with other cooked viandas such as sweet potatoes, taro root, yams, potatoes, and plantains. The sauce is also sometimes served with roast meats.

For 6–8 people

Ingredients

1 ¾ pounds cassava

For the garlic sauce:
5 garlic cloves
4 tablespoons fresh sour orange juice
10 tablespoons oil

Method

Peel the cassava, wash it, and cut into pieces approximately 4 inches long. Place the cassava in a pan and cover with water. Cook on a high heat for approximately 50–60 minutes until the cassava is tender and beginning to open up. Add salt and cook

for a few more minutes. To guarantee that the cassava softens it is a good idea to add a cup of cold water to the pan once or twice during cooking so that the process of coming to a boil is repeated. When it is cooked, drain the cassava, cut each length into two to four pieces and remove the central core. Arrange the cassava in a serving dish.

For the garlic sauce: Crush the garlic in a mortar, add the sour orange juice, mix, and finally add the oil that has been heated until very hot. Season with salt, stir well, and spoon the sauce over the cassava. Serve hot.

Chapter 7

Desserts and sweet things

MATANZAS PUDDING

Atropellado matancero

This traditional dessert of fresh pineapple and coconut glazed in syrup is a perfect example of the Cuban predilection for using fruit and sugar in sweet recipes. This particular recipe originates in the province of Matanzas, hence the name, but it might just as well be called "*habanero*," since the pineapple is the symbol of Havana. Like so many of the desserts in this country of sugar, this dish can be too sweet for some tastes but the pineapple gives it a moderating acidic touch.

For 8–10 people

Ingredients

14 ounces shredded fresh coconut
3 ounces fresh coconut, cut into ½ inch pieces
14 ounces fresh pineapple, grated
3 ounces fresh pineapple, cut into small pieces
3 ⅓ cups sugar
1 ¾ cups water
4 egg yolks

Method

Put the shredded and diced coconut and pineapple into a heavy saucepan with the sugar and water. Cook on a medium heat for approximately 2 hours until the fruit crystallizes in the syrup.
At this stage there should be a mass of fruit covered in a transparent syrup. Remove from the heat, add the egg yolks and mix well. Arrange in individual dishes and allow to cool for an hour or two before serving.

Once the mixture is cold, you can also roll small balls of it in grated coconut and serve in individual paper cases as a snack or with coffee.

BONIATILLO WITH RUM

Boniatillo con ron

Rum is the spirit produced by the fermentation and distillation of sugar cane juice, or molasses, produced in the sugar mills. Rum production is an important element in the Cuban economy and the drink is an essential ingredient at parties and celebrations. Given the important role this spirit plays in the island's life, it is surprising how little it is used in cooking.

This boniatillo is a sweet potato and syrup purée flavored with dessert wine and rum.

For 8 people

Ingredients

1 ¾ pounds peeled sweet potato
2 egg yolks
½ cup Muscatel wine
2 tablespoons 7-year-old rum
2 teaspoons ground cinnamon or 2 tablespoons toasted sesame seeds

For the syrup:
1 cup water
4 cups sugar
1 teaspoon fresh lime juice
2 pieces lime zest
1 cinnamon stick

Method

Boil the sweet potato in water for 15–20 minutes until tender. Drain and mash through a sieve.

While the sweet potatoes are cooking, prepare the syrup. Put the water, sugar, lime juice, zest, and cinnamon to cook on a high heat. Once it has come to a boil, cook for 6 minutes. Remove the cinnamon and lime zest.

Blend the sweet potato mixture and syrup together while still hot, until you obtain an even, creamy mixture. Put the mixture into a pan and add the egg yolks. Cook on a gentle heat, stirring constantly for approximately 30 minutes, until it thickens. Add the dessert wine and rum, mix well, and spoon into individual dishes. The mixture should be the consistency of a thick custard. When it has cooled, sprinkle with the ground cinnamon or sesame seeds.

Sweet potato flesh turns black very rapidly when peeled. To avoid this, peel under running cold water and cook quickly.

If you allow the mixture to become even thicker and dryer, it can be rolled into small balls when cold, coated in confectioners' sugar or crushed roasted sesame seeds, and served with coffee.

SQUASH PUDDING

Budín de calabaza

Squash belong to that group of vegetables and tubers known in Cuba as "viandas." It is easily grown on the island and can reach such large proportions that it is often sold in pieces rather than whole. Squash can also be used to make desserts, as in this recipe.

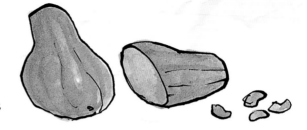

For 8 people

Ingredients

For the caramel:
½ cup sugar

1 ¾ pounds squash, peeled and seeded
7 ounces butter
1 cup water
3 cups milk
2 tablespoons cornstarch
¾ cup sugar
2–3 drops of vanilla extract
6 eggs, separated

Method

For the caramel: Melt the sugar in a pan until it is golden. Pour the caramel into a baking dish measuring 9 inches in diameter and 3 inches deep. Move the dish around in your hands so as to spread the caramel around the inside base. Allow to cool.

Cut the squash into large pieces and cook with a quarter of the butter, a pinch of salt, and the water for approximately 25 minutes. The squash should be very tender and the water completely evaporated.

Heat the milk for 2–3 minutes. Mix the cornstarch in a cup with 2 tablespoons of cold water.

Blend the squash in a food processor with the milk, sugar, the remaining butter, the cornstarch, and vanilla. Cook this mixture on a medium heat for 30 minutes, stirring constantly. Allow to cool.

Add the egg yolks to the mixture and stir in well. Beat the whites into peaks and carefully fold into the mixture with a spatula. Turn into the caramel-coated dish and cook in a water bath in an oven preheated to 350° F for approximately an hour. The pudding is cooked when a knife put into the middle comes out clean. Chill the pudding for at least 5–6 hours before turning out of the dish and serving.

> There are a number of different versions of this pudding in Cuban households. This version is less common but is lighter than many.

PAPAYA FRITTERS WITH BANANA SAUCE

Buñuelos de papaya con salsa de platano

Cubans love fruit and the island is richly endowed with many varieties: orange, papaya, pineapple, naseberry, soursop, custard apple, banana, grapefruit, melon, mango, guava, etc. ... Fruit is consumed in juices, cooked in syrup or fresh for breakfast or as a starter. Even in the nineteenth century, in his book *Cuba with Pen nineteenth Pencil*, the North American traveler Samuel Hazard noted with surprise the already prevalent habit of serving fruit as a starter at lunch. Nowadays, walking through the streets, it is common to see children sitting on the corners eating mangoes or other fruit gathered from the trees.

This recipe is not a classic of Cuban cuisine but rather reflects the new directions in cooking which seek to use local ingredients in new creative ways.

For 6–8 people

Ingredients

1 pound papaya, peeled and seeded (the fruit should not be overripe)
3 tablespoons sugar
3 tablespoons 7-year-old rum
1 cup wheat flour
½ cup beer
oil for deep frying
1 tablespoon confectioners' sugar

For the sauce:
3 tablespoons honey
3 tablespoons water
2 tablespoons 7-year-old rum
10 ounces peeled bananas
1 tablespoon fresh lime juice

Method

Cut the papaya into pieces approximately ¼ inch thick and 2 inches long. Arrange the pieces in a dish and sprinkle with the sugar and rum.

Put the flour in a bowl and add the beer little by little, mixing constantly to form a batter. There should be no lumps.

Heat the oil in a large skillet on a high heat. It should fill two thirds of the pan.

Using kitchen tongs, take a piece of papaya, dip it into the batter and deep fry until golden, then drain on paper towel. Repeat this process with all the pieces of fruit. Sprinkle the fritters with confectioners' sugar and serve with the banana sauce.

For the sauce: Heat the honey with the water and rum in a pan until it comes to a boil. Allow to cool, then blend with the bananas and lime juice until creamy. The sauce should not be prepared too long in advance or it will darken.

GUAVAS IN SYRUP

Cascos de guayaba en almibar

Fruits in syrup or crystallized are traditionally very popular in Cuba. As long ago as 1856, the author of *Manual del Cocinero Criollo* (The Creole Cook's Handbook) devotes a whole chapter to these fruit recipes.

Guava is a very aromatic fruit, rich in vitamin C. It can be eaten raw, but cooking it rids it of its sometimes disagreeable sandy texture while maintaining its aroma. This dish is usually accompanied by a mild young cheese, but it is also very refreshing served with cream.

For 6 people

Ingredients

3 ¼ pounds mature guavas
2 cups water
2 cups sugar

Method

Peel the guavas and cut in half. Remove the seeds carefully with a spoon, leaving the fleshy halves. When the seeds have been removed the guavas should weigh around 1 ¾ pounds.

Put the water and sugar in a pan and bring to a boil. Add the guava halves and cook for approximately 40 minutes until they are tender and the syrup is thick. Allow them to cool and then serve.

If the syrup is too liquid, you can remove the guava halves when they are cooked and boil the syrup for longer until it thickens.

Reduce the amount of sugar, if desired. In general, desserts in Cuba are extremely sweet.

The guava flesh attached to the seeds that have been removed can be used to make fresh juice or jam.

ORANGE PEEL IN SYRUP

Cascos de naranja en almíbar

On the northern coast of Cuba, near the city of Holguín, lies the small town of Jíbara. Formerly a prosperous port, it now seems as though time has stood still here. The state of the town's elegant houses and theatre reflects the arrival of harder times but this is not true of its people. Maria Chacón, full of refinement and culture, cares for the Jíbara colonial museum, a mansion echoing of more glorious epochs, with scarce means but as much love as though it were her own home. She has the support of neighbors like Nancy Pérez, committed to maintaining the charm, refinement, and customs of bygone times in their small but enchanting town. Maria Chacón is helped in the museum by Sara Ferrero, who, incidentally, prepares the most exquisite orange peel in syrup that I have ever tasted.

For 4–6 people

Ingredients

2 pounds sour oranges
2 cups sugar
1 cinnamon stick

Method

The sour oranges used for this dish should have very thick skins. Peel the oranges carefully, removing only the fine outer layer of orange/green skin. With a sharp knife make four incisions in the pith, dividing the fruit into equal quarters, taking care not to pierce through to the pulp. Very carefully, insert a finger at the top of the orange where the four incisions meet and peel the white skin so as to have four perfect quarters. Repeat the process with all the oranges. The pulp should remain round and whole. You should get around 8 ounces of pith quarters if the orange skins are thick enough.

Put the pith into a pan and cover with water. Bring to a boil and cook for 2 minutes. Remove from the heat, drain, refresh in running cold water, and squeeze each quarter of pith in the palm of your hand. Repeat this process two or three times to remove any bitterness from the pith quarters.

Make a syrup with 1 1/2 cups water, the sugar, and cinnamon, and cook for 6 minutes. It should not be too thick. Put the orange pith into the syrup and cook for another 7–8 minutes. Allow to cool for at least 2 hours before serving.

This dessert is traditionally accompanied by mild soft cheese.

The leftover pulp of the orange can be used for marinades or stews, or the juice can be mixed with sugar and water to make an orange drink. This is similar to lemonade and is a traditional drink in Cuba.

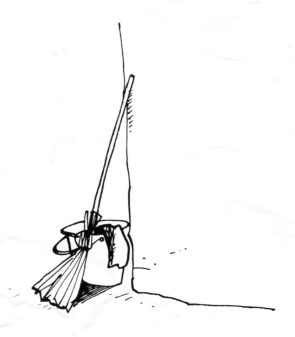

STUFFED CHAYOTE

Chayotes rellenos

The chayote (or christophene) belongs to the Cucurbitaceae family, like the squash, and originates on the American continent. In Cuba it is used for both savory and sweet dishes. It is as tasty served as a main dish stuffed with meat as it is boiled and covered in garlic sauce as a side dish. And it is especially delicious, as this recipe shows, when boiled and filled with a fine cream made of its own pulp mixed with milk, cornstarch, and sugar, then flavored with vanilla, lime, raisins, and almonds, and finally covered with cinnamon and breadcrumbs and browned in the oven.

For 4–6 people

Ingredients

3 chayotes (about 2 pounds)
¾ cup sugar
3 tablespoons sifted cornstarch
1 cup milk
3 egg yolks
1 piece lime zest
2 ounces raisins
3 drops vanilla extract
2 ounces toasted almonds
¼ cup breadcrumbs
2 teaspoons ground cinnamon
2 tablespoons butter

Method

Cut the chayotes into equal halves. Put them into a pan with enough water to cover and a pinch of salt, and cook for approximately 25 minutes once they have come to a boil. Drain and allow to cool. Remove the flesh from each half, taking care not to pierce the skin.

Mash the pulp through a sieve and mix in a pan with the sugar, the cornstarch combined with the milk, the egg yolks, and lime zest. Cook on a gentle heat, stirring constantly, for 15–20 minutes, until it is thick and creamy and has lost all taste of cornstarch. Add the raisins and vanilla. Stir well.

Arrange the chayote skins in an oven dish and fill with the mixture. Distribute the almonds among the filled chayote skins, burying them in the cream filling. Sprinkle the breadcrumbs and cinnamon on top. Dot with butter and bake for 15–20 minutes in a 400°F oven until golden. Serve hot.

> **Do not overcook the chayote or they will be too watery and soft.**

COQUIMOL

This delicate cream made of coconut milk is a traditional recipe that is eaten on its own as a custard, as a sauce with other desserts, or as a filling for pastry.

It is worth bearing in mind that cane sugar can be sweeter than sugar from other sources such as beet sugar, and since Cuban recipes intend the use of cane sugar, it may be necessary to adjust the amount.

For 6 people

Ingredients

For the coconut milk:
14 ounces freshly shredded coconut
2 ½ cups lukewarm water

2 cups sugar
1 ¾ cups water
a few drops fresh lime juice
10 egg yolks
½ cup milk

Method

For the coconut milk: Put the finely shredded coconut into a bowl and pour the lukewarm water over it. Leave for an hour, then strain through cheesecloth to obtain the coconut milk. Measure out 2 cups of the milk and set aside.

Put the sugar and water into a pan and cook on a medium heat for 2–3 minutes until it is a thick syrup. Add some drops of lime juice and allow to cool a little.

In a pan, mix the beaten egg yolks, lukewarm syrup, the cow's milk, and the coconut milk. Cook in a water bath or on a very low heat stirring constantly for 15–20 minutes until it thickens. It should have the consistency of custard. It is important not to let the cream boil while cooking or it will curdle.

Pour the cream into individual dishes and allow to cool before serving.

COQUITOS

In the 1950s, the candies made of sugar and grated coconut and known as "coquitos" were sold for centavos in the street, and often at the very gates of the school where the street vendors were always sure of finding plenty of customers.

The silk-cotton tree (*Ceiba pentandra*) is a tree of the Bombacaceae family that grows all over the island. It is the sacred tree of the Afro-Cuban Santería religion and the spirits of the dead are supposed to live in it. Believers make their offerings at the foot of the sacred tree seeking favors from the saints, or *orishas*. The offering is said to be more efficacious if it includes a centavo coin, which is why the roots of the silk-cotton tree are littered with coins. Children who had no money of their own used to run to the silk-cotton trees and secretly take the coins to buy coquitos from the traveling vendors.

For 15–20 pieces

Ingredients

12 ounces sugar
9 ounces finely shredded fresh coconut

Method

Put the sugar and shredded coconut into a pan and cook on a high heat, stirring constantly, for approximately 20 minutes until the mixture starts to come away from the sides of the pan. When cooking, the sugar turns into a syrup that coats the coconut. By the time it is cooked, it is a thick paste of coconut and syrup.

Drop the mixture in spoonfuls on aluminum foil, forming little heaps. Once cold, the coquitos solidify. The candies can be kept for some time in a tin.

> The coquitos can also be covered in caramel and are then known as *"coquitos acaramelados."*

YUCA PASTRIES WITH GUAVA FILLING

Empanadas de yuca rellenas de guayaba

These pastries filled with guava paste are a traditional Cuban dessert. The pastry can be prepared in various ways but it is particularly good when made with cassava.

Despite the popularity of cassava (yuca) in Cuba, the word "yuca" also has a pejorative sense. "Juanito is a yuca!" means that Juanito is stupid and brutish.

For 24–27 pieces

Ingredients

a quantity of cassava pastry (see Cassava Pasties, page 28)
12 ounces guava paste (see Guava with Cheese and Mint, page 120)
oil for deep frying

Method

Roll out the dough very thinly on a floured surface. Cut out circles approximately 4 inches in diameter. Cut the guava paste into ¼ inch thick rectangles. You need as many rectangles as you have circles of dough. Place a piece of guava paste onto each circle of dough and fold over into semicircles, sealing the edges by pressing hard with your thumb or a fork.

Heat the oil in a skillet on a high heat. Deep fry the pastries until golden, then drain on paper towel and serve.

PINEAPPLE CUSTARD

Flan de piña

Every year in Cuba all teenage students spend time in the famous "country schools." The purpose of these schools is to teach young people about rural labor, in what is a primarily agricultural country. The students live and work with the farmers. This experience is recalled with nostalgia by many Cubans but there are two jobs that they all remember as being horrifically hard: the sugar cane harvest and the pineapple harvest, when arms, hands, and even faces are covered with cuts and scratches from the spiny pineapple leaves.

This custard made of egg yolks and pineapple syrup is a classic of Cuban cooking. It can be accompanied by a fresh fruit salad to take the edge off the sweetness.

For 8 people

Ingredients

1 cup fresh pineapple juice (see method)
2 cups sugar
a few drops of fresh lime juice
12 egg yolks
1 teaspoon 7-year-old rum

Method

For fresh pineapple juice, peel a pineapple and remove the hard core. Cut the flesh into small pieces and blend. Sieve the blended pulp to obtain the juice.

Put the pineapple juice, sugar, and some drops of lime juice in a pan. When the mixture starts to boil cook for approximately 20 minutes, until it reaches the thread stage or 223° F on a candy thermometer. The mixture has reached the thread stage when the syrup poured from a spoon falls in one fine thread rather than in individual drops.

Pour a small amount of the syrup into a ring mold approximately 9 inches in diameter, and tilt to cover the inside of the dish with a thin film. Allow the rest of the syrup to cool a little.

Beat the egg yolks in a bowl, add the lukewarm syrup and the rum. Strain the mixture and pour it into the mold. The mixture should only fill about 1½ inches of the mold. Cover, and cook the custard in a water bath on a medium heat for 20–25 minutes. The cream is ready when a knife inserted into it comes out clean.

Allow to cool for several hours before turning out of the mold.

> When cooking the custard in the water bath, stand the dish on a rack so that it is not touching the base of the pan containing water. Take care also that none of the boiling water in the water bath can get into the dish or the custard will be spoiled.

118

COCONUT COOKIES

Galleticas de coco

There is no opulent Cuban meal that does not end with a strong, thick coffee, a glass of aged rum, and an aromatic cigar. As the poet Nicolás Guillén wrote:

And finally, a perfect end to so much food,
A small cup of steaming hot coffee…

Y al final, buen remate a tanto diente,
una taza pequeña
de café carretero y bien caliente.

These cookies are a perfect complement to either the after-dinner strong black coffee or the morning milky coffee so *de rigueur* for the Cuban breakfast.

For 15 cookies

Ingredients

6 ounces shredded fresh coconut
3 tablespoons butter
¾ cup wheat flour
½ cup brown sugar
2 egg yolks
a pinch of salt
grated zest of 1 lime

Method

Mix all the ingredients in a bowl with your hands until you have a well-mixed dough. Form the mixture into balls approximately 1½ inches in diameter and squash them gently flat in the palm of your hand.

Grease a cookie sheet with butter and arrange the cookies on it. Bake in an oven preheated to 350° F for around 40 minutes until golden.

GUAVA WITH CHEESE AND MINT

Guayaba con queso y hierbabuena

Guava paste can be considered the quintessential national dessert. The paste is made into small bars that are sometimes larded with guava jelly.

In the old days, Camagüey was the main area of guava paste production. Samuel Hazard noted in his 1870 travel book: "…One of the first things a foreigner notices in the Cuban home is the great consumption of guava with cheese, the former being in the form of either paste or jelly. The custom is so widespread that we ended up by asking what this guava was that they use it so much; and … Puerto Principe [nowadays the city of Camagüey] is precisely the place where they most devote themselves to the production of guava paste." (*Cuba a pluma y lápiz, Tomo III*, Editorial Cultural, La Habana, 1928. p.126)

Nowadays the homemade paste can be bought in the farmers' markets but care should be taken, as the paste is often made with barely refined sugar, the strong flavor of which masks the aroma of guava. The commercially produced paste sold in the supermarkets is very good quality but not as good as the one that is produced using this recipe!

For 8–10 people

Ingredients

For the guava paste:
2 pounds ripe guavas
2 cups sugar (see method)
²/₃ cup fresh lime juice

1½ pounds fresh cow's milk cheese
1 bunch mint

Method

For the guava paste: Peel the guavas, blend, and sieve the purée to remove the seeds. There should be approximately 2 cups of guava purée. Use the same volume sugar as guava purée.

Put the sugar, lime juice, and guava purée into a heavy pan and cook on a high heat, stirring constantly, for 45–50 minutes until the mixture darkens and comes away from the bottom of the pan. It is important to keep stirring to prevent any sticking to the pan or the paste will be full of blackened crusty pieces.

Line a rectangular baking dish measuring approximately 7 x 3 inches with waxed paper. Pour the hot guava paste into the dish and allow to cool for 3 or 4 hours. The fruit paste should be firm.

Once the paste is thoroughly cold, turn out of the dish and cut into slices approximately ¼ inch thick. Cut the cheese into slices the same size. Place a slice of cheese on top of a slice of guava paste and garnish with a leaf or two of mint. Serve.

In Bayamo, guava paste is presented as little packets wrapped in corn leaves and tied with string made from the same leaf. They are called *"tusitas de guayaba"*.

The cheese should not be a cream cheese but a very fresh hard cheese like Italian mozzarella or Spanish burgos. In Cuba I always prepare this dish with the exquisite buffalo milk cheese produced on the island.

CORN PUDDING WITH RAISINS AND ALMONDS

Harina de maiz con pasas y almendras

In Cuba, fresh ground corn is called "tender" corn flour to differentiate it from "dry" corn flour, or cornmeal, made from the dry kernels ground into a fairly rough powder. Various savory and sweet dishes are made from dry corn flour such as: corn flour with crabmeat (*harina con cangrejo*), cooked and seasoned with crabmeat; corn flour filled with mincemeat (*harina rellena con picadillo*), cooked with mincemeat in the middle, etc. Corn flour cooked on its own is called "*funche*" and used to be the daily fare of the poor in times of crisis. This *décima* or song-poem was popular in the 1930s when the economic recession drove many to feed themselves on *funche*:

I'm longing to taste
Some fine food
I can't stand wretched corn flour
Anymore.
When I sit down to lunch
Everything lights up
Because there are ten of us at home
And the whole table is bright yellow.

Tengo ganas de probar
alguna comida fina
porque la maldita harina
ya no la puedo pasar.
Cuando me siento a almorzar
Todo se me encandelilla
por el centro y por la orilla
porque en casa somos diez.
Toda la mesa se ve
completamente amarilla.

For 8–10 people

Ingredients

12 ounces dry corn flour
2 pieces lime zest
1 teaspoon salt
1 cinnamon stick
1 cup milk
2 cups sugar
⅓ cup raisins
⅓ cup toasted, chopped almonds
3 tablespoons butter
2 teaspoons ground cinnamon

Method

Sift the flour to remove the thickest of the grains. Wash the flour in cold water, changing the water several times. Once it is clean, the flour should be bright yellow and the water clean and clear.

Put the cleaned flour in a pan with 6 cups water, the lime zest, salt, and the cinnamon stick. Cook on a medium heat, stirring constantly, for 40–50 minutes. You should obtain a thick purée. Add the milk, sugar, and raisins. Mix well and add the almonds. Continue cooking and stirring for 30–40 minutes until it becomes a thick cream.

Remove from the heat and add the butter, cut in pieces. Mix the butter in well and pour into individual dishes. Once it has cooled, sprinkle with cinnamon and serve.

This flour retains a slightly grainy texture even when cooked.

SOURSOP CHAMPOLA ICE CREAM

Helado de champola de guanabana

Soursop champola is a popular drink made from soursop mixed with milk and sugar that came in time to be eaten as ice cream as well. It seems clear that the word "champola" has African roots. On the one hand, the word *"sampula"* in the Congo means "to stir quickly," a process that is needed in the production of this drink. On the other hand, in the Serené language of Senegal, *chambola* is the name of a certain type of melon that the slaves brought to Cuba during the colonial period which might have been applied to the soursop.

The soursop belongs to the Annonaceae family, along with other common Cuban fruits the custard apple and cherimoya. Although the three fruit are similar in flavor and can be substituted for each other in this recipe, the soursop has the finest and creamiest texture.

For 4–6 people

Ingredients

1 soursop
2 cups milk
2–3 tablespoons sugar

Method

Cut the soursop in half, remove the center and extract the pulp with a spoon. Blend the pulp for 1–2 minutes on the lowest speed so as not to crush the seeds. Sieve the mixture to eliminate the seeds and put back into the blender. There should be 2 cups of sieved fruit. Add the milk and 2–3 tablespoons of sugar depending on the sweetness of the fruit. Blend the mixture until it is creamy.

Freeze the mixture in an ice cream maker.

APPLE-FLAVORED BANANA ICE CREAM

Helado de platanitos manzano

Ice creams and fresh fruit juices have always been popular in Cuba and are a good way of fighting the heat. *"Duro fríos"* (ice lollies) are currently very popular with young people and the homemade frozen fruit juices on a stick can be bought at roadside stalls. In the old days, the Chinese were renowned for making the best ice cream; nowadays the firm of Coppelia makes the best and offers such enticing flavors as coconut glacé, pineapple glacé, orange/banana, chocolate ripple, etc.

Little apple bananas are a variety that are about half the size of a normal banana with a firm, creamy flesh that has a slight aroma of apples. However, any variety of banana can be used.

For 4–6 people

Ingredients

1 pound peeled apple bananas
1 teaspoon fresh lime juice
1 tablespoon 7-year-old rum
3 tablespoons milk
½ cup sugar
1 cup light whipping cream
2 egg whites

Method

Crush the bananas in a blender with the lime juice, rum, milk, and sugar. Whip the cream and mix into the banana mixture. Freeze the mixture in an ice cream maker. After 10 minutes freezing, stir in the egg whites beaten into peaks. Continue freezing until ready to serve.

CORN CREAM
Majarete con leche

The production of sugar, tobacco, and rum have been and still are the basic elements of the Cuban economy, to the extent that one local politician apparently commented: "We Cubans have an after-dinner economy." Indisputably the production of sugar cane for the manufacture of sugar and rum brought Cuba enormous wealth, especially in the nineteenth century. This wealth was reflected in a society that enjoyed good living and earthly pleasures, including the pleasures of the table. Traces of the past are still visible on the island in the magnificent houses: the Limoges, Wedgwood or East India Company porcelain services, the Baccarat crystal, and silver cutlery.

Corn cream, a very fine custard cream made with fresh ground corn mixed with milk and sugar, is a traditional Cuban dessert and a good example of culinary refinement in a sophisticated society.

For 4 people

Ingredients

4 corncobs
3 cups milk
½ cup sugar
2 teaspoons ground cinnamon

Method

Clean the corncobs and remove the kernels with a knife. Grind the kernels in a grinder or meat mincer until they form a paste. There should be 10 ounces of pulp.

Mix the corn pulp with the cold milk and strain through a fine sieve or piece of cheesecloth. Pour into a pan, add the sugar, and cook on a high heat stirring with a wooden spoon until it begins to boil. Reduce the heat and stir energetically while

the mixture thickens so as to avoid lumps. Continue cooking for approximately 30 minutes on a gentle heat while stirring constantly until the mixture is a smooth cream that coats the spoon and does not taste starchy. Strain the corn cream and pour into individual dishes. When cool, sprinkle with cinnamon.

Once it has cooled, the cream should be smooth and neither too thick, nor too runny. It should have a delicate flavor of corn but not starch.

If you buy the corn ready ground it is usually more liquid than that ground at home and will possibly need less milk. If you do use bought corn you should use it immediately or it acquires a bitter flavor.

This dish can be flavored with a few grains of aniseed while it is cooking if desired.

BLACK BOY IN HIS SHIRT

Negro en camisa

The name of this recipe, so politically incorrect in our times, sends us back to the era of colonialism and slavery. Black boy in his shirt is a delicious rich cake made of chocolate and peanuts. In Cuba, cocoa is produced in the east of the island and although it is not much used in desserts, it used to be customary to drink hot chocolate, a habit less common nowadays.

Peanuts are sold in Cuba unroasted in the farmers' markets and roasted in paper cones in the streets and in the doorways of theaters and cinemas. There is always a peanut seller (*manisero*) to be found on every corner. Roasting peanuts is easy: you heat them in a pan, moving them around until they become brown and the skin starts to fall away. To peel them well, once cold, rub them between your hands so that the fine skin falls away, then blow on them gently to remove any remaining bits of skin.

For 6 people

Ingredients

4 ounces cooking chocolate
4 ounces butter
5 eggs, separated
4 ounces sugar
4 ounces roasted, peeled, ground peanuts
1 tablespoon confectioners' sugar

Method

Melt the chocolate and butter in an oven dish in a preheated oven at 350° F for 15–20 minutes. Remove from the oven, mix well, and leave to cool.

Mix the egg yolks, sugar, and ground peanuts with the chocolate mixture. Beat the egg whites into peaks and fold carefully into the mixture.

Grease a round ovenproof dish measuring 8 inches across and 2 inches deep with butter. Pour the mixture into the dish and cook in a preheated oven at 400° F for around an hour. To test whether it is cooked, push a knife into the center and see if it comes out clean.

Turn the dessert out of its dish onto a rack and leave to cool. Sprinkle with confectioners' sugar before serving.

This dish was traditionally served with cream custard but it is also delicious served with Coquimol (page 114) or with Apple-flavored Banana Ice Cream (page 124).

PASSIONATE PAPAYA

Papaya ardiente

This recipe is the creation of the great Cuban chef Gilberto Smith Duquesne. Apart from working in the Hotel Riviera and the El Carmelo restaurant, both in Havana, he was for many years during the 1940s and 50s chef at the Cuban embassy in Paris. Gilberto is still going strong in his eighties and continues both to cook for friends and to work as president of the Culinary Association of Cuba. Full of sly humor, Gilberto baptized this recipe "passionate papaya," alluding to the double meaning the word "papaya" has in certain parts of Cuba where it means both the fruit and the female sex.

For 6 people

Ingredients

For the sponge:
2 cups egg white
1 1/4 cups sugar
zest of 1 lime
1 1/2 cups wheat flour
6 ounces butter

3 papayas (about 1 pound each)
6 tablespoons 7-year-old rum
3 cups banana or almond ice cream
3 egg whites
3 tablespoons sugar

Method

For the sponge: Whip the egg whites into peaks. Add the sugar and lime zest and carry on whipping until the mixture is a stiff meringue. Fold the flour in carefully with a spatula, little by little. Finally add the melted butter, mixing it in the same way as the flour.

Grease a rectangular mold, about 10 x 6 x 2 1/2 inches, with butter and sprinkle with flour. Pour the mixture in and cook in a preheated oven at 400°F for approximately 1 1/2 hours. The sponge is cooked when a knife inserted into the center comes out clean. Set the sponge cake aside to cool.

Peel and cut the papayas in half. Remove the seeds and place the halves face up on a plate.

Cut the sponge into 12 slices 1/4 inch thick and the same width as the surface of each papaya half. Put a slice of sponge into each papaya half, using your hands to press and fit the cake into the hollow of the fruit. Sprinkle 1 1/2 tablespoons of rum over the sponges in the papayas and fill each one with ice cream so that a mound of ice cream rises above each fruit half. Finally, cover the ice cream with another slice of sponge and sprinkle another 1 1/2 tablespoons of rum over them. Put the papaya halves into the freezer for 45–60 minutes.

Whip the egg whites into peaks and add the sugar. Continue whipping until you have a firm meringue. Remove the papayas from the freezer, cover them with the meringue mixture and arrange them in an oven dish. Brown under the broiler for 1 or 2 minutes only until the meringue is golden. Remove and flambé them with the rest of the rum ready heated in a pan. Serve immediately.

> The papaya halves are lightly frozen when filled so that when the meringue is cooked, the ice cream won't melt. They should not be frozen too much or the fruit will go too hard.
>
> The meringue should only be browned under the broiler so that the ice cream does not melt.

COCONUT TOCINILLO

Tocinillo de coco

Coconuts proliferate in Cuba where they have many uses, from the cosmetic creams and shampoos made from coconut oil to ceremonial use in the Afro-Cuban religion. In Santería, coconut is ritually offered to the deities, *orishas*, or it is used for divinations, when the shell is broken into four pieces.

Coconut is used in cooking mainly in recipes for candy, such as coquitos, as grated coconut in syrup, for coconut biscuits, or in this recipe for coconut pudding. There is even a drink called "*saoco*," that mixes coconut water with rum inside the coconut itself. In one part of the country, the area around Baracoa, coconut milk is used for various savory dishes as well.

For 6–8 people

Ingredients

To caramelize the dish:
5 tablespoons sugar

2 cups water
2 cups sugar
6 ounces shredded fresh coconut
8 eggs, separated
10 sablé cookies

Method

To caramelize the dish: Melt the sugar on a medium heat and stir until it is a golden caramel. Pour into a round ovenproof dish, which should be 8 inches across and about 2 inches deep, and spread quickly over the base by tilting the tin. Allow to cool.

Heat the water and sugar on a high heat and when it boils, cook for 1 minute until it is a light syrup.

When the syrup is cool, add the shredded coconut, the beaten egg yolks, and the crushed cookies. Stir well. Finally, beat the egg whites to soft peaks and fold in carefully with a spatula. The mixture does not need to be particularly thoroughly mixed.

Pour the mixture into the prepared dish and cover with a lid. Cook in a water bath on a medium heat for approximately 1¼ hours. Test by putting a skewer into the middle which should come out clean. Remove the dish from the water bath, remove the lid, and cook for 10 minutes in an oven preheated to approximately 400°F.

Turn out of the dish when it is thoroughly cold, preferably the following day. The dessert will have two distinct parts, a pudding covered with golden caramel on top and a coconut sponge beneath.

MORÓN COOKIES

Torticas de Morón

Cuba has never produced wheat, and "flour" has always meant corn flour. Wheat flour came to the island with the Spanish and was called "Castillian flour," possibly because it was grown in that region.

These little cookies are a traditional recipe from the town of Morón in Ciego de Ávila province and are made with wheat flour.

For 9–10 cookies

Ingredients

1 cup confectioners' sugar
2 cups wheat flour
½ cup melted pork fat
½ teaspoon ground cinnamon
1 pinch of salt

Method

Mix all the ingredients in a bowl until you get an evenly blended dough. Roll the dough out on a floured surface to a thickness of about ½ inch and cut out rounds 2 inches in diameter.

Cook in a preheated medium oven (400° F) for approximately 30–40 minutes until they are golden. Allow to cool before serving. These cookies should melt in the mouth.

FRITTERS IN CINNAMON SYRUP

Buñuelos en almibar de canela

Fritters made from the group of vegetables known in Cuba as "viandas" are traditionally served during the Christmas festivities. In the old days, they used to also be sold at street stalls where the client could choose between syrup and sugar cane molasses to dip them in.

For 25–30 fritters

Ingredients

1 pound peeled cassava
4 ounces peeled squash
4 ounces sweet potato
1 egg
1 ounce butter
3–4 ounces wheat flour
oil for deep frying

For the syrup:
2 cups water
2 cups sugar
1 stick of cinnamon
1 piece of lime zest

Method

Cut the cassava, squash, and sweet potatoes into pieces, place in a pan, and cover with water. Boil for around 30–40 minutes until they are soft. Drain and remove the cassava's hard central fiber.

Mash the viandas through a mincer or sieve into a thick, malleable purée.

Place the mound of purée on a floured surface, make a well in the center into which add the egg and butter cut into pieces. Knead the mixture together, incorporating the flour as well, little by little, until you have a smooth dough that doesn't stick to your hands. The exact amount of flour will depend on the quality of the vegetables, but you should only add just enough to bring the dough to the right consistency not to stick to your hands; any more flour and the fritters will be hard when fried.

Take a piece of dough the size of a large marble and roll it with your hand on a floured surface into a rope about ½ inch diameter and 8 inches long. Make a figure-of-eight shape with the rope. Repeat this operation with the rest of the dough.

For the syrup: Boil the water with the sugar, cinnamon, and lime zest for 5 minutes. Then cool.

Heat the oil in a pan on a high heat. Deep fry the fritters until they are golden. Drain on paper towel. Arrange the fritters in a dish and pour the syrup over them. They are best eaten lukewarm.

> Aniseed can be substituted for cinnamon in this recipe, and can be added to the dough as well as to the syrup.

Appendix 1

Weights and measures conversion tables

Volume

1 teaspoon = 5 ml
1 tablespoon = 15 ml (½ fluid ounce)
1 cup = 250 ml (8 fluid ounces or ½ pint)

Weight

1 ounce = 25 g
1 pound = 450 g

Length

1 inch = 2.5 cm

Oven temperature

250°F = 120°C
300°F = 150°C
350°F = 180°C
400°F = 200°C
450°F = 230°C

Examples of conversions

1 cup chopped onion = 120 g chopped onion
1 cup diced tomato = 150 g diced tomato
1 cup chopped bell pepper = 120 g chopped bell pepper
1 cup sugar = 180 g sugar
1 cup wheat flour = 120 g wheat flour

Appendix 2

Index of recipes by chapter

Side dishes 83

Avocado and pineapple salad..........................87
Black bean and pepper salad..........................90
Braised eggplant..92
Cabbage stew 83
Cassava in garlic sauce 101
Congrí rice..86
Corn fritters..94
Cucumber salad 91
Glazed sweet potatoes 89
Green plantain fufú 96
Plantain "tostones" 100
Rice with vegetables 85
Sweetcorn stew...97
Temptation plantains.....................................99

Desserts and sweet things 103

Apple-flavored banana ice cream...................124
Black boy in his shirt 127
Boniatillo with rum 105
Coconut cookies 119
Coconut tocinillo..132
Coquimol 114

Coquitos 116
Corn cream 126
Corn pudding with raisins and almonds 123
Fritters in cinnamon syrup 133
Guava with cheese and mint...........................120
Guavas in syrup 110
Matanzas pudding...103
Morón cookies 132
Orange peel in syrup 111
Papaya fritters with banana sauce...................107
Passionate papaya 131
Pineapple custard..118
Soursop champola ice cream...........................124
Squash pudding 106
Stuffed chayote..113
Yuca pastries with guava filling 117